UNION
LAKE

UNION

LAKE

Carla Porch

ARCHWAY
PUBLISHING

Cover image: *Canal des Esclaves* by Carla Porch © 2011
Interior image: *Doris's Kitchen Window* by Carla Porch © 2003

Archway Publishing books may be ordered through booksellers or by contacting:

Archway Publishing
1663 Liberty Drive
Bloomington, IN 47403
www.archwaypublishing.com
1-(888)-242-5904

Union Lake is a work of creative nonfiction. Although place names have been retained, many of the characters' names have been changed.

ISBN: 978-1-4808-0215-5 (sc)
ISBN: 978-1-4808-0216-2 (e)

Library of Congress Control Number: 2013914690

Printed in the United States of America

Archway Publishing rev. date: 10/02/13

For my parents, of course, Carlton and Doris

Now you say you're leavin' home
'Cause you want to be alone.
Ain't it funny how you feel
When you're findin' out it's real?

—"Sugar Mountain" by Neil Young

CONTENTS

Preface

I Lie on My Father's Side of the Bed (December 2002)

I LIE ON my father's side of my parents' bed. He has long since passed away—twenty-seven years ago this coming February. It is now between Christmas and New Year's, and tonight my mother was rushed from Genesis Rehabilitation Center, where she had been recovering from the aftermath of recurring small strokes, to the local hospital. She suffered another one soon after I left her when visiting hours ended. Her attending nurse found her on the floor, unable to speak or move. Tests will be performed in the morning to determine the extent of the damage caused by this last stroke. On Christmas Eve my mother's physician had assured me the blockage in her carotid artery, the cause of the strokes, could be reduced through medication. If she could maintain the physical therapy regimen, she would be strong enough to go home with assistance from a visiting nurse soon after the New Year. Until tonight her brain damage had been slight and physical therapy had worked. Earlier today she strolled down the halls of the center without a walker. Afterward, as we shared Christmas cookies, she said, "God, I can't wait to get out of here and sleep in my own bed."

My mother's side of the bed still waits for her return.

WHEN I WAS growing up, my father would gravitate to his side of the double bed he shared with Mom after watching the evening news on *The Huntley-Brinkley Report.* That corner of my parents' bedroom functioned as his office. It was his place to smoke, read, do crossword puzzles, and re-render plans of yachts and sailboats he had built—but had not designed—during the day at Colonial Boat Works. Stacked along the wall were the books he planned to read, had read, or was reading at the time.

Other times my father typed on a portable Smith Corona he stored in its box at the far side of the nightstand next to the bed. The nightstand had two drawers. The top one housed a carton of Camels, always with one open pack on top, a box of matches, drawing pencils (in varying degrees of hardness), erasers, and a compass. Smells from lead, flint, and rubber underscored the more prominent tobacco bouquet. The deeper bottom drawer contained larger drawing tools: a mechanical ruler, a triangle, and a French curve on top of a box of typing paper. Barely noticeable on the far side, under the overhang of the triangle, were two books: *Candy* and *Plexus*. I knew these were dirty books. Why else would Daddy have hidden them in a drawer?

Daddy would sit on the side of the bed, open the top drawer of the nightstand, take out three previously sharpened lead pencils of #3, #4, and #5 hardness, and lay them down in that order on the top surface, along with a red rubber eraser and a compass. He put an open pack of unfiltered Camels and a book of matches next to a large square, glass ashtray already in its place in the other corner close to him. Next, he set his self-made, portable drawing board (it matched identically the commercially made bedroom furniture) and a T-square, which hung from the board, on my mother's side of the bed. Grabbing his pillow, he propped it up against the headboard and pushed his back against it. He then put the drawing board over his long thighs that were stretched out on the bed. From the bottom drawer, he took out the French curve, the triangle, and a sheet of paper, always one at a time, and slipped the paper under the tiny metal catches in each corner to secure it to the board.

To begin drawing a boat, Daddy placed the mechanical ruler vertically to calculate plot points, first along the right side of the sheet and then across the center, in barely visible pencil marks. The T-square clicked in place on the left side of the board as the pencil moved horizontally along the paper, letting out a "swoosh" as it formed a line. After two more clicks, the T-square hit the side of the board again, and the triangle met its arm. The long fingers of his left hand grabbed their juncture and held the T-square firmly as his right hand moved the pencil up perpendicularly to create a mast. The French curve and #4 pencil followed with a bow and stern.

My mother used her side of the bed for sleeping only.

As I LIE on my father's side of the bed, the aroma from the maple finish on the drawing board, the lead from the sharpened pencils, and the tobacco are still here. I find myself back at the Genesis Rehabilitation Center, talking with my mother's nurse, the one who had called to tell me my mother had another stroke. We stand next to the bed where my mother sleeps, each holding a vial of clear liquid. The nurse pours hers into an open section of a small machine attached to the wall above the bed, and the fluid crests to the top without dripping over. I pour my vial into an adjacent section, but I pour too much and the clear liquid runs down the wall and onto the floor. Overcome with embarrassment, I drop the glass vial. The shattering echoes throughout the room, and I flee. My feet smash glass shards all the way down the hall as I skirt around patients in wheelchairs and others holding onto walkers with IV drips attached to their arms. When I push through the front door, a carnival parade is passing under the breezeway, and the revelers sweep me into their wave of movement toward the parking lot without anyone grabbing onto my arms. I am apprehensive, but I don't resist.

A drumbeat begins and then a few more, which are followed by many short, continuous waves in succession. I don't see drummers, but the beating emanates from all around me and resonates within my body. The crowd propels me forward, and a throng of brown and tan faces—neither distinguishable nor recognizable—encircles me. A flaring, flaming red skirt on a woman, whose face I try to make out, and many men in khaki pants and white T-shirts bop up and down to a samba. More featureless women dressed in wide skirts of brilliant turquoise, fuchsia, and chartreuse join in from the side. Ubiquitous smiles glisten as shoulders move forward and back while feet follow suit. With every several beats, a whistle blows followed by a few more drumbeats; metal hits metal, sounding like the carriage return of a typewriter. I look up at the dark night sky and see the Milky Way, unobstructed.

The samba procession leaves the parking lot and enters a dirt road leading into the forest behind the center. Off the hard pavement, the unrelenting carnival power diminishes. I veer off from the side of the road without the dancers noticing I am no longer with them and turn around and run on a narrow, sandy path. I recognize this path; it will lead me to the woods behind my mother's house—I know how to get back home.

Without having come into the house through the kitchen entrance, as I would have if I had been awake, I am back on my father's side of the bed. Slowly, I inhale the acidity of the paper and the lead from the drawing pencils inside the nightstand no longer here. I feel safe as I awaken, but I miss the peace of mind my father had created when he placed calculated dots on a page like stars in the sky with his pencil and then connected them to create a constellation.

PART I

Origins in Great Sound

"Hurry up! The tide's going out," Aunt Alice calls from far away.

Mom catches a lightning bug. A light blinks through her squished-together fingers.

"We can't dillydally. Uncle Bob is waiting for us," Mom says. "He wants to take us out on his boat to watch the full moon rise."

A lightning bug flies in front of my face, and I try to grab it with one hand.

"You have to grab with two hands and keep them cupped together," Mom tells me. She can hold a lightning bug between her two hands and walk fast down the path.

I follow one bug into the tall grasses alongside the path. The soft, muddy earth grabs my sneaker, and I can't keep up with the bug. Then the smell holds me in place. I get happy when I am with that smell. It stinks the most when the tide goes back to the other side of the world. Aunt Alice said it goes to a place called England. I close my eyes and let the mosquitoes bite me.

"Where are you, wild Indian? I see the top of the moon," Aunt Alice yells.

One foot comes up with a sneaker still on, but the other is naked. I dash out from the grass, holding the dripping, muddy sneaker.

"What happened to your sneak?" Mom calls from inside the boat when she sees me running up the little bridge. She picks me up and sets me on the ledge so that my legs dangle over the side.

"The muck tried to swallow it," I say. Aunt Alice kisses my forehead as she pours a big jug of water over my muddy foot and then on the muddy sneaks that she holds in her other hand. I sit still and breathe in the salty fish and gasoline smell. I don't like the gasoline part. Gasoline smells dirty, but it makes the boat run, and I love riding on the boat because it takes me to the clean, salty fish smell.

Uncle Bob turns on the engine. Aunt Alice puts a life preserver on me while I jump up and down barefooted. She pats my bottom, and I run to sit at the front of the boat, where I can't smell gasoline. The salty, fishy wind blows up my nose and tickles me all the way down to my toes.

Mom scoots next to me and asks, "You're still my tadpole?" I had taken a long time to come to her and Daddy. She had to live at the seashore and swim every day in the ocean all summer long before I would grow inside her.

The boat engine roars and Uncle Bob steers toward the rising moon.

Princess Tinkling Water

DADDY SITS ON the back step and whistles to a bobwhite in the big oak behind our house. I scrunch up next to him. He knows how to speak to birds in their own language and smoke a cigarette at the same time. The bobwhite calls back. Their whistles sound alike.

He points to a large tree stump at the edge of the backyard and says, "That's where I found you. One night when I was trimming the lilac bushes, I heard a whimper from the woods. The old Indian that hangs around here must have left you in the stump."

I shake my head "No" and lean on his knee while looking over at the stump. Daddy's a big tease. No one else has seen the old Indian but him. Everyone says I look like an Indian because of my dark brown plaits, but we know I really am not.

I jump on his lap, hug his neck so tightly he makes a choking sound, and yell in his ear, "No, the old Indian didn't leave me there. You're my daddy."

When we can't take the mosquitoes biting us anymore, we go inside. Daddy sits at the kitchen table, and I stand next to him. In front of us is a jar of round, smooth, plastic beads and a ball of string. Daddy cuts a long strand from the ball.

"That should be long enough," he says. He measures it around my head, cuts another, and then two more, all the same length. He unscrews the lid from the jar and slowly pours the red, yellow, blue, and green beads onto the center of the table. He knots the end of the string to keep the first bead from falling off and picks up a yellow bead and threads it. Red, green, and blue follow. He hands me the rest to string. "Don't go all the way to the end with the beads because we need enough string to make a knot and tie the two ends together."

After each string is beaded, Daddy lays the four strands next to each other, cuts another string from the ball, weaves them together into one piece, and then braids the string ends into one. He brings my plaits from behind my shoulders to the front and circles my head with the band of beads.

"Now there is no question you're an Indian," he says. Daddy cuts another string from the ball, but not as long as before, and wraps it around my neck for size. "Got that right," he says and cuts four more. He gives me two strings, and together we bead yellow, red, blue, and green. "Squaws always wear wide-collar necklaces, so we'll make this wider than the headband," he tells me. After weaving the five strings together, he ties the beaded collar around my neck, and then he cuts another string, this time even shorter. "Show me your left wrist, Princess Tinkling Water. Since you are right-handed, it's best to wear the bracelet on this wrist, so it doesn't get in the way when you draw and write. And not as wide—just three strands."

A Haircut in the Kitchen

WHEN I WAS three, Mom brought me to Bonnie's Beauty Salon.

She told Bonnie, "I don't like to hurt her." Bonnie said a pixie cut would fix that, and then there would be no more tears from me—at least, not from combing out the knots in my fine hair.

When it was time for Daddy to come home from work, Mom told me to hide behind the armchair near the kitchen doorway.

"As soon as your daddy walks through the door, jump out and yell, 'Look, I'm a big girl now.'"

After Daddy walked in, he turned to Mom and said, "What the hell did you do to her? She looks like a goddamn boy."

By four I was in pigtails. By five I was in tight long braids, one on either side of my head.

THE WARM MORNING breeze off Union Lake came through the living room window and billowed the sheer curtain panel into Mom's face. She grabbed it and pulled it to one side and then leaned her palms on the sill. Her long, thin nose nearly touched the screen as she peered through the oak and pine grove out front, across the baseball field, and into the backyard of one particular house close to the dugout. I knew where Mom's eyes were going because I stood right behind her.

"I don't see his car," she said while turning around to face me, "so Larry is still around."

It was Labor Day.

Larry parked his black convertible Jaguar XKE behind his mother's house during the week while he worked as a beautician in Greenwich

Village. He kept the Jag there because he said it was more fun driving it around our South Jersey back roads than on New York City streets. After coming down by bus on Saturday, he would sometimes stop by in the Jag to see us, and, if she needed it, to shape up Mom's bob. I knew that of all her nephews—and Mom had several to choose from—Larry was the one she felt the closest to, and I think Larry felt the same toward her. He only asked about his other aunts and never mentioned visiting them.

Mom had asked Larry a few times whether he wanted to open his own shop in town, although she knew a man working as a beautician would be considered a sissy; only women were beauticians here, and only men were barbers, and we knew Larry was not a sissy. She thought he would do well because he was understanding and had a pleasant way about him, and more importantly, she knew he would give women the haircuts they asked for because he always gave her the haircut she wanted. Mom assured him all his aunts and her friends would be his customers.

"I don't think so, Aunt Doris. It's easier to be myself in New York," he replied, adding that coming down here on weekends was enough for him.

"Stop bugging him about moving down here. He makes bigger bucks working up in New York," Daddy said after Larry had left the last time she had asked. Mom never asked him again. I don't think Daddy had a problem with Larry being a beautician, nor would he have ever called him a sissy. He liked Larry a lot, though I wondered if Daddy was protecting him from those around here who refused to understand that a man could do a woman's job. Daddy knew how to do women's work. Everyone knew he was a better cook than Mom. His lasagna, goulash, and homemade bread still remain the best I have ever tasted. He invoked sweetness in his cooking without using sugar, and he embroidered, knitted, and crocheted too. But Daddy didn't make a living doing women's work; he built boats.

Mom dressed me in floral or checkered short sets in pink, yellow, blue, lavender, and green from late spring to early fall. Sometimes we even dressed alike. Larry always dressed in black, even in summer.

As soon as he'd walk through our kitchen door, and before he even had a chance to sit down, Mom would hand him a glass of iced tea and ask, "Doesn't that black shirt and slacks make you hotter?"

Larry always responded with a chuckle and said, "No, Aunt Doris, I'm just fine. In fact, I'm quite cool." He was one of the few people I knew who could chuckle and speak clearly at the same time.

In winter Mom would ask Larry if he was going to a funeral. He always quipped back, again with the chuckle, "Yeah, and who died?"

When the weather became warm enough, Larry would give me rides in his Jaguar, top down. It too was completely black, and it was the only car I had ever been in that roared. When it stopped at stop signs and traffic lights, it purred. When it was parked, it resembled a ready-to-pounce jaguar, like the ones I had seen on *Wild Kingdom*. I had been in a sports car before. Another cousin, Jack, had an old black Dodge coupe he had turned into a hot rod. It was fun to ride in, because Jack drove fast, but the coupe sputtered and it didn't resemble an animal. I sat so low in the seats of Jack's car that I could barely see out of the windows.

When I rode in the Jaguar, the wind would pick up my braids, making them fly behind my head like streamers in suspended weightlessness. Most of the time my plaited hair made me feel anchored to the earth. Even the fastest bike pedaling I could muster or sliding down the long slide in City Park could not come close to the Jag soaring down the hill on Sharp Street Bridge. Maybe riding a roller coaster would have given me the same sensation, but I was afraid to ride roller coasters back then. The only time I felt that kind of freedom was when I rode in Larry's Jaguar.

Sometimes Larry and I would stop at Blinker's Custard Stand. Once I asked him if he thought soft vanilla in a cup with peanut crunch on top was boring. Everyone in my family—Mom, Daddy, aunts, uncles, and cousins—thought it was. They considered me a fussy eater but put up with me because I was the baby of the family—the youngest of all the cousins by many years, and my parents' only child. This time I thought I would try butterscotch on top instead. If I didn't like the butterscotch, I wouldn't eat it; I didn't want Larry to pay for something I didn't eat.

"It's your choice," Larry said. "Eat what you want. If you don't like the butterscotch, you can go back to your usual." I had four favorite cousins, but Larry was definitely the best. I tried the butterscotch, and I liked it.

THE JAG WASN'T in its parking spot. That meant Larry had stayed the extra day, running around somewhere. We called it "running around" because we didn't know where he went in the Jag. He never said, and we never asked. Mom had told me, "Larry is private. He has to be, because his mother is such a nibshit."

A nibshit is South Jersey for a nosy person. Later, when experience and geography had expanded my vocabulary, I would define it, more specifically, as a cross between a nitpicker and a yenta. Aunt Lucy was Mom's ex-sister-in-law; Larry was named after his father, who was my mother's brother. He had divorced Aunt Lucy long before I was born and died when I was three, so I don't remember Uncle Lawrence.

Mom had said many times her brother Lawrence would never be dead because his son was his "spitting image"—tall, husky (Larry had been a quarterback in high school), and dark. Larry's olive complexion had come from Uncle Lawrence's father, who was Jewish. Mom and Uncle Lawrence were really half-brother and half-sister. He was a baby when his father died, and Mom's dad had raised him as his own. Uncle Lawrence had been Mom's favorite brother.

After an hour or so, Mom picked up the receiver and dialed the telephone; the Jaguar had returned to its spot.

When the receiver on the other end answered, Mom said, "Lucy, it's Doris. Is Larry around?"

"OUCHIE," I CRIED. I sat on the tall stool near the kitchen sink, watching *Casper, the Friendly Ghost* from the TV in the living room. It felt like Mom was pulling my hair out of my head with her barber's comb. She parted it in a quick, downward swoop from behind my bangs to the nape, and then grabbing one half, she pulled it over to the side, pulling harder than usual. Using her free hand, she turned on the kitchen faucet and ran the comb under the water. Mom always dampened my hair when she wanted the braids to stay in longer than usual.

"These have got to be real tight. I don't want to have to pull out ticks stuck to your scalp after I come home from Marie's," she said. "Remember when I had to use a hot match and tweezers because the ticks wouldn't let go." Mom had let me have just a single ponytail while I played outside that day. The ponytail had become loose—so loose it really wasn't a ponytail anymore. She had found about five ticks when she brushed my hair before washing it that night.

Mom was leaving me with Daddy after he came home from the

boatyard at lunchtime; he worked half days on Saturday. She was going down to Wildwood along with her sister, my Aunt Alice, to stay overnight with their friend Marie at her beach house. This would be their last get-together at the shore until next summer. Daddy and I knew that besides going to the beach to get a tan and a swim in the ocean, they went nightclubbing. That's what the three of them did when they were together. Mom said it was the only time she had a chance to drink a Tom Collins—her favorite cocktail—in peace, and she loved to dance. Mom always came back from Marie's beach house in a good mood.

After Aunt Alice picked up Mom in her station wagon, the rest of Saturday, like always, was a blur of climbing trees and running around in the woods behind our house. Some of the time I was by myself, and sometimes I was with the kids from the neighborhood. Nothing memorable ever happened, and nothing bad ever did either.

Before going to bed, Daddy and I agreed that he had to let out my braids, because I looked like I had been electrocuted. A network of wild, wispy hairs had pulled away from the braids and surrounded my head. Bits of tree bark clung to the loose strands and grains of sand stuck to my scalp. As Daddy unraveled the braids, picked off bark, and rubbed out sand, the locks fell in ripples down my back and around to the front of my torso.

"Are there ticks?" I asked just in case.

"You're clear."

"Do I have to wash it?" I asked.

"Nah, I got all the dirt out." I felt his fingers continuing to rub my scalp, and then he added, "I'm not going to brush it either because that will take out all the waves." He laughed when I told him I was growing my own mohair sweater but without the itch. Since that one pixie cut, my hair had grown in rather straight. Mom still called it baby-fine, except I wasn't a baby. Now, for the first time, it was full and fluffy.

The next morning Daddy read the entire Sunday *Philadelphia Inquirer* and did the crossword puzzle in the magazine section while watching *Meet the Press* and *Face the Nation*. He was too busy to braid hair, although he did know how and had done mine once when I was in kindergarten and Mom had gone to the hospital to have a varicose vein removed from her leg. He had done my braids so tightly that they stood out on either side of my head.

"Let's wear it loose for a change. We never get to see the beauty of your hair, since your mom always keeps it braided," he said over breakfast, which we had at lunchtime. He gave my head a once-over with a brush, ignoring the small knots forming at the nape. Last night's ripples had relaxed to their usual straightness.

"Get your suit on. We're going up to the lake for a swim before the Phillies game comes on," he said while we put our dirty lunch dishes in the sink. We both forgot about my loose hair. He also forgot to take me to Sunday school, and I forgot to ask to go.

When Mom walked into the living room that night and saw me sprawled on the carpet in front of the television watching *The Wonderful World of Disney*, she cried, "Never again," to no one in particular. She yelled over at Daddy, who was on the couch reading, this time Esquire, "How could you?"

Back on the tall stool in the kitchen, I cried the entire time Mom brushed the knots. Her one hand grabbed clumps of hair close to their roots, while the other hand brushed feverishly, ripping through the matted clusters at the other end. Hair brushing was the only time Mom ever hurt me.

At some point she asked, "Don't you think it's time for a big girl's haircut? You'll be going into third grade on Thursday."

I really didn't know if it was time. I loved how my hair had fallen over my shoulders and down my back the night before. It had hugged me with its wetness when I'd gotten out of the lake, and its sway was intoxicating.

Daddy couldn't put in his two cents because Mom was so angry with him, but he wouldn't apologize either.

The only thing he said was, "Jesus Christ, all I did was let her have her hair loose for a change. She looked pretty."

Mom snapped back, "Well, she doesn't look pretty now."

The next morning my roots still really hurt. I had answered the big-girl haircut question last night with a sniffled "Maybe." I was worried I could look like a boy.

DADDY HAD TOLD me once about his first haircut. He had been six years old. Back then boys didn't get their hair cut until after they had started school. He had natural banana curls, unlike the ones Mom made for me with curlers for special occasions like Easter. Mine lasted for about an hour, because my hair wanted only to be straight. It was hard for me to imagine Daddy with long black curls since he was nearly bald, with only a circle of gray hair around the sides and the back of his head.

Nobody made fun of a little boy with banana curls in kindergarten, but when Daddy went into the first grade, the situation changed. All the little boys who'd had long hair in his kindergarten class now wore their hair short.

"First grade is the beginning of real school," Daddy had recalled, "so the other boys' moms had cut their hair. My mom hadn't yet—partly because she worked all day in the mill and had four other sons to look after. Her real reason, though, was she thought my curls were too pretty to cut, and none of my brothers had curly hair. On the first day of school, the boys in my class called me a girl. I ran home at lunchtime and told my grandmother, who looked after us while my mom worked. She said, 'We can't have that,' and she cut my hair. I returned to school for the afternoon session looking like the rest of the boys in my class."

Daddy continued. "What was funny is that nobody else—my older brothers, relatives, or the kids I played with around my house—ever called me a girl. It took my mom a while to accept me in short hair. Though she was a young widow, she never wanted to remarry, and so Mom knew she would never have a girl. I suppose having me in long curls was the closest she could get to having a girl."

I could trust Larry to cut my hair and not make me look like a boy.

LARRY PLACED THE tall stool in the center of the kitchen. After I sat down, he draped his hairdresser's cape over my shoulders and wrapped a thick, red rubber band at the top of my long, single braid, which had taken four years to grow. As he cut his way through my thick hair just below the rubber band, his barber scissors made a hacking sound. Once all the hairs were severed, I felt a force leaving from behind my head.

Mom grabbed the detached braid from Larry's hand and said, "Your Grandmom Smith believed saving hair brought good luck," and then she put it in a clear plastic bag.

While Larry styled my now chin-length hair into a pageboy, his silver chain-link bracelet jingled. I asked him what he did in New York besides cutting hair. He said he went to nightclubs and heard folk singers like Peter, Paul, and Mary.

"They sing *Puff, the Magic Dragon,*" Larry said.

I quipped back with, "I know that."

Then he knelt down, held my head straight, and looked into my eyes and up at my bangs.

Mom scooted alongside him and said, "Can you do something about that cowlick? I've tried. I've even taken her to her father's barber to have him try fixing it."

Larry held down sections of my bangs with his fine-tooth comb and said, "I'm not cutting your bangs straight across like your mom does, but along an angle, like the beatnik girls in the Village."

From the corner of my right eye, I caught the sparkle from the diamond ring on his pinky finger and told him—and I don't remember why—"I'm going to live in Greenwich Village when I finish high school."

Talisman

FEAR FOLLOWS ME all the way to the top drawer. I am at a place forbidden to me, but it's too late to turn back. I have come too far not to get what I have set out to take. I open the drawer, and the scent inside hits me, holding me in place. Just one whiff and I freeze, right there in front of the nightstand. The smell always comes before I even see what is forbidden. Actually, I am stealing, taking without asking, but the smell takes me first, and also without asking. For a brief moment, a voice inside my head asks, "How can this smell have so much power and make me do what I shouldn't be doing?"

The panic dissipates as the aroma moves quickly up my nose and down behind my throat to settle on my tongue. It takes my breath away, and my nostrils respond by opening wider to this peculiar sensation. There's a mild hurt, a slight discomfort, though not quite unpleasant. I can taste the pungent smell. Pungent is bitter with a little sweet, except this pungent becomes mostly sweet after the second whiff.

Mom says, "Sometimes you crave bitter like you do sweet."

The sweet part feels good too.

I assure myself, "It's okay to take what doesn't belong to you." Relaxation transforms fear into fearlessness, and I focus on the sweet.

The tobacco is stronger today. I can smell the earth it grew in, along with fertilizer and dried cow manure, like the kind my aunt puts on her flowerbeds and tomato plants. I forget I am scared—or should be. Daddy must have opened the pack this morning. He has smoked only two or three so far, and that makes it easier for me to take two more without it being noticeable. The pack will still look almost full. If he catches me, though, God knows what he would say. Mom would guilt-trip me with,

"You should be ashamed!" Then she would ground me for weeks on two counts: stealing and smoking.

"Come set the table," Mom calls from the kitchen.

I have seconds to take what I am there to get. Together, right pointer finger and thumb grab two cigarettes and pull them out at once, without lifting the pack from its corner.

I whisper to the drawer, "Please don't squeak," and quickly grab the handle with my left hand to close it.

A Sleepover on the Delaware Bay

My BEST FRIEND Shelley—on again/off again since fifth grade—invited me down to her grandparents' caravan trailer at the Hacienda Campground on Delaware Bay. Shelley has met a guy named Mark there, who comes down most weekends from Philadelphia to stay with his dad and stepmother. Mark considers Shelley his girlfriend and writes to her practically every day. In his last letter, he requested she bring a friend for his friend Matt.

How can I lose? I am contending with a face covered entirely with pimples and a lopsided Mary Quant hairdo that is taking forever to grow out. I realized too late, after my hair was cut, I wasn't that kind of groomed girl. In the past year I have had four barely memorable boyfriends. None of them really attracted me, but since I feel unattractive, they have filled the gap while I pray the Fostex soap clears up my face and my hair grows long again.

Pop-Pop drives his Chevy station wagon in front of the trailer, while Shelley surveys the playground across the road to look for Mark. We help unload the back of the station wagon since it will become our bedroom for the night. Within seconds we're done and move onto the swings in the playground. As our swings go up and down, a blond figure and a dark-haired one emerge from a grove of cedar pines. Shelley introduces me to the blond Mark, and he responds by introducing us to the dark Matt. Immediately, Mark pulls Shelley over to a bench and they go into their own private conversation. Matt and I give each other a little smile. I stay on the swing and twist its chains together in a clockwise rotation. When I can't go one more revolution, I pick my feet up off the ground, spin counterclockwise, and end up facing Matt. Behind him in the distance, I see Nanny standing at the picnic table next to the trailer yelling, "Girls!"

Shelley cringes and says, "It's time to eat. We have to set the table." The four of us agree to return to the playground after dinner.

When dinner is over, we pick up the dirty dishes off the picnic table and take them into the trailer without being asked. Shelley washes; I dry and put the dishes back into their small cabinet. She squeezes the water out of the sponge and sets it on the windowsill; I stretch the damp dishtowel evenly over the rack. Shelley opens the screen door for us to leave, and I gently guide it closed.

As we run over to the playground, Nanny, nestled in a cedar grove with other campers, calls from her beach chair, "Thank you, girls."

The fireflies are the first to greet us. Mark grabs Shelley from behind and puts her on the seesaw. I go back to winding myself up with the chains of the swing while Matt stands in front of me, telling me he's getting his driver's permit next year. He's been saving the money he makes at the Acme supermarket near his high school to buy a decommissioned ambulance to refurbish. I'm thinking that's weird. It's over three years till I'll qualify for my license, so I don't say much. Then it's dark and Shelley tugs at my arm.

"We got to go make our bed in the back of the wagon." We agree to meet Mark and Matt on the beach again at midnight.

Shelley and I lie in the back of the wagon on a mattress fashioned from wool blankets, sweating and swatting mosquitoes that have snuck in through the small window opened for ventilation. The mosquitoes' wings create the only breeze as they buzz by our faces. Despite these discomforts, our time passes quickly as we debate what base I'll get to with Matt, or he with me. I'm embarrassed to ask Shelley what base she has gotten to with Mark. He's almost a year older than Matt and acts so sure of himself. Shelley becomes rather quiet around Mark; I think she has gone to more bases than she cares to admit, and I admit I'm a bit of a prude.

With large dark eyes set into an angular narrow face, Matt has a minimal amount of acne—way less than me. We conclude that he may have a total of four pimples. These flaws are compensated for by the soft rose tint to his cheeks, which says, "Kiss me." His sharp features make his nose seem a bit large and his teeth too.

"Those teeth could get in the way if you ever kiss," Shelley says.

I come back with, "But his full, tulip-shaped lips help conceal them."

His hair is wavy and slicked around his ears. His father has forbidden him to have long hair; Matt is determined to grow it down to his shoulders, however. The only way he'll cut it is if his draft number comes up when he turns eighteen, but that's over two years away.

The color of Matt's eyes and hair makes him look Italian, or maybe Jewish, though his complexion is either English or Scandinavian. Then it hits me.

"Shelley, he looks like George Harrison."

She sits up and says, "Yes! And you're half English!" She turns to look for the flashlight behind the tire well on her side. Shining the flashlight on my Timex, she adds, "So, you two have a lot in common."

The time is 11:50 p.m.

Shelley slowly opens the back passenger door on her side while I pretend we're agents on *Mission Impossible*. She knows how far to open it before the door squeaks.

I slide across the bottom sheet, place my feet on the prickly grass, keep my "ouch" to myself, and then turn around and fluff up the top cover. If Nanny checks on us, it will look like we are lying there. Shelley pushes in the handle button and soundlessly closes the car door. Our bare feet tread on pebbles and clamshells covering the road alongside the shower house where we stop to pee. We hobble back on the road and start giggling, because we're walking around in baby-doll pajamas and wondering what we will say if we get caught. Ahead, two figures, backlit by a half-moon, stand in front of a waveless bay.

Mark's arm encircles Shelley's bare shoulders, and he walks her down the beach, where they disappear inside an anchored dinghy. I stand at the edge of the water, gazing over at the pinpoint lights in Delaware and then up at the cloudless sky. In all my thirteen years, I have never had an experience like this one: a clear sky with moon, Milky Way, and constellations viewed without obstruction. The moon highlights minuscule waves in the bay while their tiny movements tickle my submerged feet. I turn, and Matt is on my left. His moonlit shadow has eclipsed mine. My arms cross over my upper body in an attempt to conceal my braless breasts. He comes over to me and puts his right arm around my shoulder, and we walk up the beach along the glistening line where water meets sand. The tide is going out, so we have a choice as to what driftwood to sit on. We pick a long tree trunk with its dried roots still intact.

For the next few hours, we don't move from our spot. Matt's right hand caresses my shoulder while his left holds my hand, but no kissing. He has stopped talking, and I'm getting sleepy. When is he going to kiss me? He's taking a long time, and I'm not going to make the first move. I never have, not yet. I'll wait. I like him. He's lean but muscular, and he smells nice. I like that smell. It's not from deodorant or aftershave—it's human.

Though the sky remains dark, I sense the sun coming up and hear the tide returning. I break from Matt's caress, turn around to look behind me, and see a faint light through the marsh grass. I dread having to go over to Shelley while she is making out with Mark to tell her we should get back before Nanny or Pop-Pop notice we're not in the back of the wagon. Instead, I sit back down and into the notch between Matt's chest and shoulder. He gently grabs my chin and pulls my face toward his. His lips barely touch mine, but it's a kiss—not a French kiss, just a dry, soft one. His teeth do get in the way at first, but my lips find a way around them.

Four weeks later in Stone Harbor

THE OCEAN WAS truly special that day in early September. I just couldn't get enough of it—my last swim until next year. My body's temperature and the ocean matched perfectly, no adjustment necessary. When it was time for us to leave the beach and get back to the campground, I couldn't. With every rise to the surface for breath, I saw Nanny waving for me to come onto shore. But I kept riding the waves in and then immediately swimming back out to where they were formed, followed by underwater somersaults while waiting for the next one to ride. As I dove down to sit on the ocean floor and watch waves roll over my head, Matt followed and kissed me on the mouth. Finally, a wave landed me close enough to shore so that I could break away from the pull of the ocean and stagger over to Nanny.

She threw a beach towel around me and said, "I'm renaming you Sea Turtle."

PART II

Got Miller?

The bottom drawer

MY MOTHER REFERRED to his typing as just typing. She never said, "Oh, your father is writing a poem, a letter, or a book." She simply said, "He's typing." I don't know whether she was consciously thinking of Truman Capote's famous one-liner about Jack Kerouac when she would say it— probably not. But it might have been something she heard on a talk show that had just stayed in her head. They both used to watch a lot of talk shows—*The Merv Griffin Show*, *The Dick Cavett Show*, and *The Tonight Show*—and Truman was a frequent presence, his squeaky baby voice shooting out poison darts at anybody whose writing or fashion sense he didn't like.

Daddy's keystrokes could be heard anywhere in the house, even out in the backyard. Dressed in striped boxer shorts and a white undershirt—a T-shirt in winter and sleeveless in summer—he became entranced by his typing.

Daddy typed in bed at night before he went to sleep. I could never understand how he managed to keep his legs spread apart with the typewriter in between for as long as he did, particularly with the typewriter stacked on top of its box, and both together resting on a wobbly mattress. Sometimes he typed on Saturdays too, if he didn't have to go into Colonial Boat Works, where he built yachts and sailboats. On Sundays he watched sports on television, or he worked on smaller boats he built on the side, either up at Union Lake or behind our house next to his wood shop. I never asked, "Daddy, what are you typing?" Something kept me from being the one to break the spell he was under. I don't think he would have told me anyway.

For a brief period at eleven years of age, I stole cigarettes, two at a time, from an ever-present open pack of filterless Camels that sat on a carton in the top drawer of Daddy's nightstand. I usually took them as soon as I got home from school, while he was at work and my mother was preparing dinner in the kitchen. He smoked so many cigarettes that those in the pack never grew stale, since the pack would not be open for more than two days. Only fresh tobacco aroma infused the drawer.

After pulling out the two cigarettes, I laid them next to the large glass ashtray on top of the nightstand, making sure the slightly less-filled pack was in the same position as Daddy had left it. I would then move to the drawer below, containing a box of typing paper and two books: *Candy* by Maxwell Kenton and *Plexus* by Henry Miller.

I had just moments to scan for sexy parts in these two dirty books Daddy thought he kept from sight. My mother could appear at any moment or yell from the kitchen for me to set the dinner table. All the scenes in *Candy* were sex scenes, or at least they seemed so to me. I had assumed *Plexus* was a dirty book too. Henry Miller was telling a story about himself, I thought, since he wrote in the first person. But there wasn't just one sex scene after the other; I had to scan through the hundreds of pages of small type to find a dirty word like "cock" or "cunt." I never could figure out what Miller was writing about.

The lid was always on the typing paper box. Once I looked under it and saw typewritten words, but I didn't have enough time to read what had been typed; the fear of my mother's presence looming from the bedroom doorway and demanding what I was doing in my father's nightstand kept me from going further. If she caught me, not only would she grill me, but she would also ground me—a dreaded punishment I had avoided in my life so far.

"Lately the pack seems to have less cigarettes than what I had smoked," Daddy said to me one day. He knew it wasn't my mother who was pinching. She smoked about three cigarettes a day and called herself a social smoker, because she would smoke only with someone else who was smoking. She kept her filtered Winstons close at hand in a small purse made specifically for a pack of cigarettes, and it made a loud snapping sound whenever she opened and closed it. So I never considered taking a cigarette from her, and besides, since she smoked so few cigarettes, I thought she might keep track of how many were in the purse.

My response to Daddy was, "I don't know."

He warned, "Well, make sure it's not you."

My brief period of stealing Daddy's Camels had already ended before he inquired if I knew why his cigarettes were disappearing. The last time I had looked, the lid on the typewriter paper box had been askew, concealing *Candy* and *Plexus*, and allowing typewritten words to peek from the opening. I took out the top sheet. These words read like those in *Plexus*. I could go no further than the first page. Like Henry Miller, Daddy had typed the word "cunt," surrounded by sentences I couldn't understand.

The locked cabinet

IT WAS A hot, thunder-and-lightning Saturday afternoon during a July Fourth weekend with nothing to do and nowhere to go because we didn't own a car yet. My husband and I had gone down to my mother's house by bus that morning from New York, where we lived in the East Village. Even if it had stopped raining, we couldn't have gone for a swim over at Union Lake across the way, because it had been closed indefinitely due to arsenic contamination.

My mother and I decided to play 500 Rummy. My husband did not know how to play the card game, and he wasn't interested in learning. If it had not been raining, he would have been patching the roof, caulking the storm windows, or painting the sills or the siding on my father's shop, which had become our—that is, my and my mother's—odds-and-ends storage room.

When my husband doesn't have something to do, he becomes unbearably antsy. He paces. So while my mother made us iced tea, I perused my father's collection of hardbound classics, displayed behind the upper, locked, glassed-in section of the living room secretary. My mother continued to refer to them as "your father's good books": Balzac, Baudelaire, Flaubert, Zola, Dickens, Shakespeare, Tolstoy, Wilde, Whitman, Emerson, Thoreau, Poe, Hemingway, and a complete set of *Funk and Wagnalls* encyclopedias from the 1940s. All remained where he had left them before he died.

I asked my husband, who lay on the sofa, attempting to nap, "How about reading an Edgar Allan Poe short story or Hemingway's *For Whom the Bell Tolls?*"

He said, "Poe isn't calling. Remember I already read your father's *For Whom the Bell Tolls* and didn't like it much. I want something other than classic."

Though my mother mourned my father's death, she removed his possessions from their bedroom soon after the funeral. She had put his drawing tools in a flat cardboard box and placed it on the top shelf in the hall closet, and she had thrown or given away all the paperbacks stacked against the wall on the floor near his side of their bed. Most of the paperbacks had been of the pulp variety. The Salvation Army had acquired his nightstand and his clothes. There hadn't been Camels around for at least two years before his death; he'd required an oxygen tank to breathe by then.

I took the key from the top of the secretary and unlocked the wooden door to a cabinet below. I hadn't been down there in years. Inside was a plastic bag filled with last year's Christmas cards and one paperback, *Plexus: The Rosy Crucifixion* by Henry Miller. I giggled to myself; my mother kept a dirty book. Instantly, the thrill of sneaking peeks in *Plexus* at my father's nightstand returned. At eleven I had not known the significance of the front cover stamp. It said "Complete Paris Edition Now Published By Grove Press," an allusion to its provocative content, welcomed by only the French.

I opened to the introduction and read it in silence. Here in *Plexus*, Miller would recount the most crucial period of his life—stretching from the moment when he made the commitment to becoming a writer at the age of thirty-three in New York City, through the next few years, and leading to his flight to Paris. There he hoped to fulfill his artistic aspiration and be released from American Puritanism. He believed he had experienced a form of crucifixion and resurrection during those years. Though it wasn't his intention to write a trilogy, *Plexus* became the second volume of *The Rosy Crucifixion* trilogy, preceded by *Sexus* and followed by *Nexus*.

"A goodly part of the narrative has to do with my struggle to express myself in words—I started late!—my difficulties in earning a living, the fight with my own complex being, my encounters with other men and women as a 'roving cultural desperado,' and so on. And more than anything, perhaps, my effort to understand the pattern of my life, its purpose and significance."[1] These last lines stood out.

I went over and sat at the edge of the sofa and continued on, reading the opening paragraph aloud to my husband: "In her tight-fitting Persian dress, with turban to match, she looked ravishing. Spring had come and she had donned a pair of long gloves and beautiful taupe fur slung carelessly about her full, columnar neck. We had chosen Brooklyn Heights in which to search for an apartment, thinking to get as far away as possible from everyone we knew ..."[2]

My mother shuffled the deck on the kitchen table, and I got up off the sofa. Before handing *Plexus* over to my husband, I remembered what a wise teacher once told me: the last word in the text of a book will give the key to what the story is about. *Plexus* concludes with "everlasting."

The billowing banner

TWO DAYS REMAINED to complete an assignment for a graduate writing class I was taking at the International Center for Photography, and I was next on the docket to read. I was beginning to doubt whether this was the right time to commit to a graduate-level class and had avoided reading over the last couple of sessions. I felt ill-equipped, because I could never set aside enough time to write without interruptions, which ranged from everything necessary for raising a small child, taking care of a home, and working part-time as both a photographer and graphic designer. But my writing teacher, who had also been one of my photography teachers, assured me I was equipped. She had admired my writing in the visual diaries I had created in her photography classes. The pending assignment was to write a letter to a favorite writer.

Although I was always reading something, I had not acquired a "favorite writer" in a while. During pregnancy and while caring for my infant daughter, I had exhausted a collection of Gabriel García Marquez, but "Dear Señor García Marquez" or "Dear Gabriel" didn't feel right; I had not developed that kind of affinity for him. Since I had no work scheduled for the next two days and my daughter would be going to day care anyway, I would use my ability to meet deadlines "no matter what"—a necessary skill for graphic designers—and just come up with an addressee.

As I pushed my daughter in the stroller around Grand Army Plaza to the day care center on the first morning, a large red banner attached to the Brooklyn Library façade billowed in the wind. "Brooklyn Library Celebrates Brooklyn Writers" it proclaimed with the names Walt

Whitman, Marianne Moore, Isaac Bashevis Singer, and a few others. *Why not Henry Miller?* I thought. *Is it because he is still viewed as the "roving cultural desperado" in the eyes of the library's banner committee?* I felt annoyed and disappointed with the library. In any of Miller's autobiographical novels, he boasts of coming from Brooklyn ("I am a patriot—of the Fourteenth Ward, Brooklyn," he says in *Black Spring*). Brooklyn provided the fodder for his best stories. My letter would be to Henry.

It took me nearly two days to complete a two-page letter. When I attempted to read it aloud to practice for class, my voice repeatedly broke. I couldn't even get through the first paragraph. With less than three hours remaining before the class, I called my friend from up the street.

"Jan, I start crying after three sentences, and no one will understand what I am reading. You have to read my letter," I said, pleading. She worked at home as an interior designer and could give me only ten minutes, because she too had a deadline that afternoon.

Jan spoke into a cassette player as ink dried on the floor plans she was rendering; she didn't sound like her usual self—cheeky and a bit rough. Two hours later, the class sat in a circle around the player listening to a smooth, collected feminine voice reading my letter on tape.

November 21, 1991

Dear Henry,

Plexus was next to the open pack of unfiltered Camels in the top drawer of my father's nightstand. I was home alone and felt free to indulge. The power of your words and the tobacco in the Camels had been too strong for me; I was eleven at the time.

My father had been a small-town boy who took to the road during the Depression. Through guile and craft, he was able to get jobs throughout the United States, Central America, and the Far East. His travels opened him up to other worlds. He returned to the small town/small life with a matured heart and embellished soul. I heard from relatives his stories were enchanting. Rigoletto would bring tears to his eyes, and invariably, he would be reading Dante or Flaubert.

When I entered his world, his life was heading into a downward swing. I suspect it was the inclusiveness of the small town. He had exhausted his remaining brilliance on pool and pinochle at the local bar, but I never saw that side of him either. Instead, I saw an angry man who surrendered to nonstop Camels, Budweiser, bad diet, and bad attitude. Internally, ulcers consumed his stomach, and breathing became a determined, conscious act of survival because his lungs no longer had the capacity to automatically provide oxygen to fuel his brain. As a teenager I didn't understand how to weigh his deteriorating health and internal struggle against his anger. The process of whiting him out of my life had begun. At seventeen I left home. My leaving, I thought, was an act of survival. He died when I was twenty. His death was my relief. I had believed it broke any remaining ties to our relationship.

Later, when I was twenty-six, while visiting my mother, I wanted something to read. Stored in a locked cabinet under a grocery bag filled with last year's Christmas cards was *Plexus*, in paperback, "Paris edition." My eyes stayed glued to the text, and I asked my mother for permission to take it back with me to New York.

Henry, it was reassuring to read you lived for years with your book in your head and that it took even longer to transcribe into literature. As I learned to unravel your narration, I gravitated to the succinctness of your literary criticism and your inclusiveness (Nietzsche and Lao Tzu in one phrase!), along with your frank eroticism and the accounts of your day-to-day life, whether in New York, Paris, or California. I took this all as paternal assurances.

With every book of yours that I read, I began to see how much my father had been like you. My compassion for him began to grow as I slowly recalled the manuscript in the bottom drawer of his nightstand. The text had been typed on my father's Smith Corona, and he was the only one who could type back then, so the words on the page were his. But it was his erotic language that stopped me from reading further. The eleven-year-old me could not accept her father's ability to express sexuality, or even to think that he was a sexual being. There was an invisible taboo rubber-stamped across the page.

Somehow, through your words, Henry, and the recollection of the forgotten manuscript, I've learned to connect with a father I could finally accept but never knew.

He Had the Green Thumb

Summer began by mid-May in Brooklyn and continued relentlessly into the middle of fall. Steady, high temperatures and infrequent rainfall made it necessary for me to go into my garden daily. During the succeeding five months, I watered, picked off dead leaves and dried-out blossoms, replanted and pruned awkward overgrowth, and pulled out stray clover and other weeds. In previous years the well-established perennials and few annuals planted over Memorial Day weekend had required only watering every other day, and less if there had been a downpour. "Deadheading" flowering plants had been the extent of my other gardening duties.

Since summer temperatures endured through October, flowers continued their summertime bloom, and leaves held back from browning beyond what would be expected for the time of year. These temperate conditions brought confusion to the perennial plants programmed for autumn's decline and winter's reprieve. The strawberry plants continued producing fruit, while the pansy tree sprouted springtime buds and then a second round of foliage. When heavy rains hit at the end of the month, bringing cooler temperatures, the garden's extended vitality rapidly spiraled downward, and I felt myself pull away. Rather than go outside to evaluate this decline, I observed it from my bedroom window, the room in my apartment with the most comprehensive view of the garden.

The garden's shift, I hoped, was toward dormancy and not death. Most of my plants grew in clay pots and whiskey barrels. Only the pansy tree grew in a large wooden planter, and the ferns in a concrete one, attached to a corner of the wall I shared with my neighbors. Each planter rested on a concrete floor and was surrounded by concrete walls. None of my plants grew in the expansive and insulating earth. Their only protection from the impending, freezing cold came from the nourishing soil surrounding their root ball, held in place by a pot or other container. Though it was so bright out there most of the day that my garden appeared as if it had full sun, it did have shady corners. So the amount of sun a plant needed to thrive determined its placement on the concrete floor.

In early November, the weather returned to unseasonably warm temperatures. As I went over to the sliding glass door to let the balmy air inside, I noticed the willow had begun to wilt; it needed water immediately. Once I turned on the hose, I could see the pansy tree and the bamboo were thirsty as well. The willow and the bamboo had grown so large over the summer. Now oversized for the wooden whiskey barrels where they grew, they would require transplanting into larger planters in the spring. The warm weather had nudged their roots to seek moisture and resume growing, despite the seasonal decrease of sunlight and the cold weather from two weeks back, which should have sent a signal for their leaves to drop.

I proceeded to water three heuchera bushes, because a new round of shiny, deep burgundy leaves covered their crests. A deep orange blossom had popped out on the geranium—a first since I'd planted it in July. I hadn't had good luck in the past with planting flowers in the middle of summer, and this one had dropped all its blossoms as soon as I had placed it in a clay pot. For the next three months, it had just been a clump of healthy green leaves, with no sign of ever blooming again. It too had overridden the finality of the chilly weather in late October.

AT THE TOP of the stairs, on a bookshelf leading into my office, rests a photograph of my deceased father. Whenever I reach the landing before turning into the main space, he greets me from this perch with a bouquet of lilacs in his hand. However, I don't always look back.

He stands erect beside the cottage he built, the home I grew up in, with a cocky grin—like Clark Gable in *The Misfits*. His full lips firmly grip a fresh-lit cigarette, and his eyes have a preening, seductive quality. I wonder whom he is beguiling—someone standing nearby or the unknown photographer behind the camera? Daddy appears to be in his element. His right arm falls at a ninety-degree angle across the front of his torso, exposing a pronounced bicep line, whose definition was created, not by lifting weights, but by years of cabinetmaking. The manly hand points to nothing apparent. Whenever I reach the top of the stairs and happen to look up at my father, I long to have known this man who had such vitality.

All I had wanted to remember about my father at his funeral were his hands—the only part of him I could bear to look at as he lay in the casket. They had been placed across his lower abdomen so that the tips of his middle fingers touched. Despite fifty years of working as a carpenter, their beauty survived. Nor had these hands succumbed to the aftermath of the diseases that had shrunk the rest of him. At death, Daddy's hands remained those of a young man.

My father and I had not made our peace by the time he died. Though nearly twenty-one years old, a junior in college, and a married woman, I remained angry with him at his funeral. Four years earlier he had forced a breakup with a boy whom I had loved—and continued to love, though I had married someone else. Soon after the breakup with the boy, I had turned to drawing and painting to fill the empty space inside me. When I showed my father my first oil painting, he asked me, "What's your point?" I didn't answer then because I had never thought, nor had I learned in class, that painting required the artist to have a point.

My mother stood by the casket, where she could hold onto the top of my father's fingers. Every so often she would kiss his forehead, and when a mourner approached with quiet condolences, she would sob. The mourner would touch my father's arm or his hand, give a prayer, place a kiss somewhere on his face, and maybe even softly cry. My father's ashen skin clung to sunken cheekbones, far too sunken for me to place a kiss on them. I remained standing at the foot of the casket, like a sentry on watch. An occasional tear rolled down one of my cheeks. An intermittent glimpse up toward his face broke my stare from his folded hands. Only once did I attempt to comfort my mother.

The two-hour wake seemed to have no beginning or middle. When the end came, a single line formed for one last look before the casket was closed. In the center was a group of female cousins older than me and mostly from my mother's side. They were clustered together in front of my father. Each stopped to hold my father's hands and then placed a kiss on his forehead or on the emaciated cheek closest to them. I could only watch. My cousins looked at him with love; they knew the man holding the lilacs.

As SOON AS my father had finished the construction on the cottage that would become our home in the spring of 1947, eight years before I was born, his hands moved on to create a backyard paradise. He planted corn, tomatoes, lettuce, onions, peppers, summer and winter squash, lima beans, and pumpkins. Then there were the flowers: forsythia, pansies, tulips, carnations, roses, marigolds, peonies, irises, gladioluses—my mother's favorite—and lilacs. My parents' half-acre sat close to the shores of Union Lake, a threshold between the southernmost point of the sandy New Jersey Pinelands, which could not sustain much more than the indigenous pitch pines, scrub oaks, sassafras, briars, and clumps of crab grass, and the fertile farmlands beyond. Local farm lore claims the Delaware Indians cultivated tomatoes hundreds of years before the British settlers arrived in what is now Salem County and twenty miles west of my parents' land. The British, in turn, introduced this luscious fruit to the rest of the world. According to my mother, my father grew the tastiest tomatoes in all of South Jersey. He could coax verdant life out of poor soil.

My father also grew the most fragrant lilacs, particularly the bush he planted by the side entrance to the kitchen. He had purchased four lilac saplings from a mail-order nursery in South Dakota and planted two purple and a white one along the far side of the house in order to demarcate his property where it bordered the neighbors' field—he felt a fence was not neighborly. On the side of the house where he posed in the photograph, near the kitchen entrance to the cottage, he had planted the remaining sapling. It grew to be rounder than the others, maturing with deeper purple blossoms, and its scent seemed almost too much. My mother would recall how he'd always received compliments for the fragrance from company passing by the bush, and then he, in return, would respond with a small bouquet from it. No doubt the lilacs he holds in the photograph came from that bush. I can still smell those lilacs when I look at him now.

MY FATHER WORKED six days a week, constructing and finishing the interiors of yacht cabins for Colonial Boat Works, a business in our hometown. For most of his eight-hour workday, his six-foot-two-inch frame crouched into a raw space, installing cabinets, adding trim, and fitting in dining benches that served as storage chests and tables that flipped up to make space for pullout beds. Daily, he inhaled sawdust from oak and mahogany, fiberglass shards floating in from construction performed on the outside of the boat, and smoke from his unfiltered Camels.

In the spring of 1954, my father took a leave of absence from his job to repair and restore sailboats at a marina in Stone Harbor, a small beach resort on the South Jersey shore. He was forty-six years old. I don't remember how he was able to take the four-month leave of absence. My mother was a housewife, so she was free to join him, and they had no children yet to consider. They had been unable to conceive, and were resigned to not having children of their own. Neither did they consider my father's garden; he let it go fallow.

Stone Harbor was about thirty miles from where my parents lived. They closed down their cottage in early May, having found a one-bedroom apartment overlooking a marsh near the marina. There was no need to drive anywhere. Food shopping was two blocks east, and the ocean another four—life in Stone Harbor was easy. My mother swam daily in the ocean, and she spent her evenings looking at the setting sun across the spectacularly green, open meadow, afterward dancing at a nightclub called Henny's with my father. They returned home in early September.

The following spring I was born. My father had returned to cabinetmaking during the previous fall—but never to gardening.

My mother told me it was an unusually mild spring day, warm enough to have the windows open, when I was brought home from the hospital after my birth. Though it was still April, the lilacs were in full bloom. My parents' bedroom was on the side of the cottage next to the three bushes. In the eight years since their planting and the two since their last pruning, the bushes had expanded beyond their allocated space. Aromatic blossoms pressed against the window screen, and the impending dense foliage would be the view until the leaves fell in autumn. My mother positioned my crib next to the window. When I no longer slept in my parents' bedroom, I would lie across the foot of their bed on a warm spring day when the windows were open and take in the redolent lilac fragrance.

I would like to think my father didn't smoke when he worked on his garden in the evenings after supper. How could he, if he dug earth with a shovel, hoed rows to plant, submerged seeds in soil, knelt to pull weeds, and stretched string into lattice for bean vines to follow, while whistling in conversation with a bobwhite who sang whenever he was around?

During the twenty years I spent with my father, he was always "not well." His body gradually became a trap. A herniated disc prevented him from performing heavy labor; stomach ulcers reduced his body weight, causing him to look frail and skeletal; emphysema robbed him of oxygen, as well as fostering asthma, so that a single whiff of intense scent from a blossom or perfume would cause him to choke; and accumulative arteriosclerosis eventually stopped his heart. When I sold my mother's cottage, twenty-seven years after my father's death, only bushes remained in his once-extensive garden: a row of forsythia, a clove spice, and the four tenacious lilacs. Crab grass covered the ground.

I SPENT MUCH of this past summer working on the dining room table that overlooks the garden, rather than in my office, so I didn't encounter the photograph of my father very often. Then, at the end of September, I resumed working upstairs in my office. While I was looking for a book from the shelf above the photograph, our eyes met. His had diminished to undifferentiated dark sockets. The gray hues of the image had muddied to brown, and the detail had softened or disappeared. Since this eight-by-ten enlargement was not a photographic print, but a computer scan of a fragile three-by-four snapshot, I should have known the resolution wouldn't hold up. The fading process had caused the now lighter background to contrast further with the amorphous foreground. The sun's trajectory, high overhead, now backlit my father, causing sharp angles of light to fall off his shoulder and onto the bouquet in his left hand, not spotlighting the lilacs I remembered but instead the zinnias, a summer flower. My eyes went to the light behind him. Deep in the background, the midday sun illuminated the entire backyard he had cultivated. I discerned rows of mature tomato plants. How could a disintegrating image reveal what really had happened? The original must have been taken in August, months past lilac season.

MY MOTHER VISITED me in Brooklyn on a warm Indian summer weekend in October, three months before her death. Together we stepped into

CARLA PORCH

my patio garden and sat down to savor the warm afternoon sun. She admired what I had been able to achieve in such a small space with soil only in pots and planters. My mother had never gardened. She considered gardening to be yard work, and therefore a housekeeping chore. Mowing what had become crab grass was enough for her—a duty she had fulfilled herself until these last few years. When the sun's warmth dwindled to cooler dusk, we went inside. Before I closed the sliding glass door, my mother grabbed my hands and held them together as she always did when she wanted me to listen.

"You have your father's green thumb," she said.

Now it is early December, and snow blankets the dead annuals and dormant perennials. A dusting clings to grass plumes, the tall bamboo shoots, and the remarkably enduring green-foliaged willow. My garden is beautiful in a surreal way. I could never have predicted this, because I have surrendered control of it. I can see beyond the collection of clay pots and wooden containers with dead leaves at their bases. I too have entered dormancy—a gardener's standstill. When the snow melts and all the leaves have fallen, I tell myself that then I can sweep, gather, and remove what has fallen to the concrete patio floor.

Indian Summer

―――――――――――――――――――――――

"FIND A SPOT that's comfortable," my boyfriend called out. Descending rays hit my right shoulder full force and showered my back with their radiant, relaxing late-afternoon heat, reinforcing his command. Knees to chest, arms hugging thighs and calves together, I found my balance on a bumpy tree stump. He didn't want me staring directly into the camera and allowed only my eyes to move. They moved to the left, and through the grove of bare trees ahead I saw a white sheet flapping behind my house, a portion of Mom's second round of wash. She never left anything on the clothesline this late in the day. At lunch she had said, "I caught good weather today." Her first round had dried before noon. The sway of the sheet held me in place.

Mom and I had agreed it was time to take a new photo of me. In the last few years, the only portraits she had were those taken at the photo booths on the boardwalk down at the shore. When I had handed her the black and white strips, she would always say, "How do you expect me to find a frame small enough for such a tiny photograph? I can barely see that it's you."

My boyfriend yelled from behind the camera tripod, "You got to keep still." He liked how the sunlight reflected on the lake and dappled my face. I gave attention to my breath and then took in the sounds around me and looked for something else to keep me still on the stump. I knew that if my self merged with my breath, like when I swam, then I wouldn't worry if my expression was right. I was breathing, I was still, and my expression would result in an image I'd want remembered.

A dried leaf rustled on the sandy, hard ground. I looked down to follow its scratchy trajectory as I held my breath. Sunlight reflecting off the lake glared into my right eye while its warmth burst across my cheek from below. I tried not to squint. Exhaling, I let my eyes return to the swaying sheet, but it was gone.

UNION LAKE CAN be seen through a sparse grove of blackjack oak, pitch pine, maple, and sassafras in front of the house where I grew up. This was the view from the living room and from my bedroom windows. No matter what else might be in the immediate foreground, the lake and the grove comprised the perennial backdrop.

The original swimming beach was up a sandy road at the end of the street I lived on. It was here I had swum during the summers until I was eleven. The sandy road paralleled a canal that served to drain parts of the lake. There were two other ways to the beach: a path through a pine barren forest and a gravel road (used more by automobiles than pedestrians) that went directly to the sailing club and the few houses at the head of the lake. When I was twelve years old, a housing developer bought the beach and the houses around it. The swimming beach was relocated from its original site at the end of the sandy road to the lakeshore on the other side of the grove across from my house.

Along this edge of the lake had been a collection of one- and two-story clapboard houses, a community created without planners or architects in the late nineteenth century. Everyone called them "the boathouses," although they were not really floating structures but bungalows built on pilings over the lake. In those days there was no beach, so to swim, one would have to jump off the dock attached to a boathouse. Some owners came from as far away as Philadelphia and even New York, though most were local folk. No one lived in the boathouses year-round because they were neither insulated nor heated.

My parents knew everyone on that side of the lake. Some were more than summer neighbors to them; they were actual friends. On warm evenings, now and then, my parents would walk through the grove and along the dirt road in front of the boathouses. They would join in conversation with these boathouse neighbors sitting among the trees after their evening meal. The older boathouse people would watch the sunset from screened-in porches, while others fished off the side of their deck, and there were those who would hop into a canoe or onto a sailboat.

The lake was always tranquil at this hour but with enough breeze for an evening sail. On weekends artists would come from out of town and set their easels in front of the boathouses, capturing a likeness on large sketchpads or canvas.

"What is special to draw or paint here?" I wondered when I was old enough to question this sort of thing. It had always been just Union Lake to me.

THE GLACIERS EXPANDING from Canada during the Ice Age never made it this far south, because their rocks and boulders stopped many miles north, where the Pine Barrens trek begins in Central Jersey. There is no glacial marring or mauling, and the land is flat and mainly composed of yellow, coarse, pine-barren sand. The new beach was created, not by lapping waves, hard rain, or the rare-appearing hurricane, but by multiple chainsaws. First, the summer boathouses were cut down, and then the pines, sassafras, oaks, and maples scattered in the front yards. Backhoes finished the job by pulling out bungalow pilings submerged into the bottom of the lake and tree stumps left in the front yards and grabbing whole saplings from out of the ground. These became lifeless stacks, as if for their own pyre.

I tried to resist watching this destruction, but when the exposed sassafras sap smell trailed through the wind off the lake and into my open bedroom window, the fragrance drew me outside. From the front yard, I stared through the grove and saw dark red clumps clinging and dripping from the roots of saplings. Were the trees bleeding? Then I realized this was not blood but, rather, the red clay layer below the yellow sandy surface. Before, I had seen only tree roots when a tree was being planted or transplanted into the ground or on a clipping after it had been rooted in water. This scene made me feel unsettled and sick to my stomach; I had never experienced desolation before, nor had I ever seen a wasteland. Now there was one across from my front yard. After the dump trucks had carried away the massive felling, the smell of sassafras lingered for days.

IN THE SUMMERTIME, my mother, and sometimes my father, would take me on the short journey to the swimming beach, usually in the late afternoon or early evening after supper. At the end of my street was the Duck Pond, which opened up to Union Lake, where the canal originated. Two of the three ways to the beach began next to the pond. Rarely would we walk through the forest; instead, we would follow the sandy road adjacent to the canal.

First, we would stop and say hello to Jimmy McGill, my dad's third cousin, who would be outside repairing a fishing boat on the pier. He ran the Union Lake Fishing Club. Then it was Mr. Peoples, sitting on his porch concealed behind darkened screens. The only evidence of his existence was the puffs of smoke emanating from his pipe. My mom greeted the smoke with, "How are you, Mr. Peoples?" The reply was always "Fine, and you, Doris?"

Mamie Vaccara would be loading fishing gear into her canoe docked along the canal. She liked to fish after working all day assembling shirts at the Model Blouse sewing factory. I'd run up to her, telling her it was four, three, or two more years till I could get my ears pierced. She would drop her pole in the canoe, turn, and say to me, "The time will be here in no time," and then kiss my forehead. She was interested because she was the local ear-piercer. My mom had promised me Mamie could pierce my ears for my twelfth birthday.

By the time we arrived at the beach, my red, slip-on Keds would be weighted down with coarse, yellow sand that had found its way inside. I'd drop the beach towel from around my neck, kick off the Keds, and descend slowly into the lake. It always felt cold at first, even in August. My dad had told me underground streams ran under the floor of the lake.

Mom would sit on the beach talking to someone, because she always knew everyone. Daddy would walk over to the closest house on the beach. It was a small cottage with a wraparound screened-in porch; it belonged to his friend Tom Price, who lived there only in the summer, while the rest of the year he lived somewhere in Florida. I think he may have been retired. Daddy and Tom, who were avid readers, exchanged books with one another. They belonged to the At-A-Boy Club, which was a combination fishing and poker club, although Mom would add "drinking club" to the description. Tom's cottage was the At-A-Boy's clubhouse. He usually lived alone.

I loved being in Tom's cottage, particularly on the wraparound porch. It was both inside and outside at the same time. I could hear the lapping waves from there, because they were just a few feet away. Sometimes, if there weren't any kids on the beach or in the lake, I would sit on the porch with Daddy and Tom and listen to their talk. One year Tom brought a Seminole woman up for the summer. She was the most beautiful woman I had ever seen in person. Her straight, shiny black hair hung down her back into a point and met at her waist, and she listened more than she spoke. Afterward Mom said she was poised and wondered what she was doing with an old man like Tom. The beautiful Seminole didn't stay for the whole summer.

Daddy would leave Tom's and walk up the beach to check on a kayak or a canoe he was building in the wood shop next to Aunt Becky Smith's hotdog stand. Once submerged, I swam on my back. Sometimes the lake breeze would carry the aromas from Aunt Becky's kitchen over to me.

When I was ten, my parents allowed me to go swimming with a friend instead of them. We sometimes took the path through the forest to the beach. It was quicker but also scarier. No one lived along the path, and few people ever walked on it. Sometimes, without asking my parents, I went alone.

MY NEXT-DOOR NEIGHBOR, Aunt Evelyn, holds my hand. We walk on the dirt road in front of the boathouses. She's not really my aunt but treats me like my real aunts do. She never had children, but we get along. I run ahead of her, grab two hanging ropes, and flop down on the wooden seat swing in front of the boathouse belonging to Mrs. Fitch, Aunt Evelyn's friend. I can see my house through the grove on the other side of the dirt road. My hands can barely make it around the thick jute tied to a big branch of the oak above. I gaze up and think the acorn that made this tree must have come from an oak in the grove and then rolled over here. But this oak is far bigger than those over by my house. I want to ask Aunt Evelyn why this oak tree is so big, but she grabs the swing seat from behind, brings it up to her face, and then pushes it forward, so I forget to ask. My legs go straight out, and my hands grip the prickly jute as tightly as I can. After a while, Mrs. Fitch waves from her doorway and says to come over. I know she's giving us a treat. I am not sure if this is her swing, because everybody from the boathouses uses it, even some of the grown-ups.

Mrs. Fitch places a plate of warm chocolate chip and oatmeal cookies in the center of the round table. She and Aunt Evelyn drink tea. I get a glass of milk. Inside, the walls are knotty pine and the ceilings are so low that Mrs. Fitch's head nearly touches. Slippery rag rugs cover the uneven floorboards. My legs dangle over a wooden chair, and I swing them back and forth. I feel dry heat on my back as it comes up from the little oven behind me. Even though it's warm outside, I like this feeling. Tiny waves slap the pilings, but the sound they make coming up through the floorboards is so loud I can't follow what Aunt Evelyn and Mrs. Fitch are talking about. I take a chocolate chip cookie and turn in my seat, so I can see around the staircase going up to the second floor and look out through the screen door. Two sunfish sailboats cross each other, and a man rows a canoe between them as breezes blow the sheer lace curtains around the wingback chair next to the door. I close my eyes and try to keep a soft chocolate chip from melting in my mouth. A motorboat passes by, and then the waves slap the pilings of Mrs. Fitch's boathouse even harder and louder. She and Aunt Evelyn laugh together. I smell the lake drift up through the floorboards; it smells like the cedar trees growing along the canal.

SAND FROM AN unknown ocean beach was spread over the leveled land before the summer season began. Its bright white glare shone through the grove and over to my street. The few surviving oaks, maples, and sassafras provided shade. Only local residents were allowed to swim at the new lake beach, and we were required to wear tags demonstrating our residency. Nonresidents were prohibited from entering what was renamed Union Lake Park. Lifeguards were stationed from nine to five during those summer months. From then on, every summer someone would drown—a rare occurrence up at the old, unguarded beach during the summertime. My mom used to say, "Sometimes it's best to leave well enough alone."

Though the community could not stop the housing development, this man-made beach could not be forced on us. Our helplessness transformed into defiance. No one from around Union Lake Park purchased the required beach tags. Many of us put aboveground pools in our backyards. My parents and other neighbors would go up to the old beach after the construction crew left or over to the new beach after the lifeguards' duty ended, since no one with authority was around to check for beach tags. I swam in our backyard pool.

During the following year, the developer acquired rights for additional land from the city to expand the housing development further out from the old beach, as the first round of land parcels had sold out. More parcels were needed to fulfill the demand for imitation baronial-Tudor mansions and French-country cottages. This next wave of reclamation would take away most of the woods behind our house; these woods connected to the forest along the old swimming beach. The developer had made an arrangement with the city to put a boulevard-type road, to be named Sunset Drive, through my aunt and uncle's property further into these woods. The road was deemed the formal entrance to the expanding housing development called Union Lake Shores.

My Aunt Alice and Uncle Bob, who had been my second parents, had a cottage nestled among the same trees as were in the grove; it was situated right behind my house. Though we would remain close, to visit one another after they moved away required a five-mile drive. Their new home was next to a forest on the other side of town; they were the kind of people who needed to be surrounded by trees. Those of us on Canal Street were allowed to stay, but those along the canal had to relocate, except for Jimmy McGill. He continued to run the Union Lake Fishing Club.

An incurable sense of displacement fell upon those of us who remained, since we would never learn to accept our changed lake community. Our collective spirit withered, and what remained of our unity was sinking; the surviving forest had become forbidden. Even an Indian summer's special light and delicate, warm air did not provide a reprieve from our mental dislocation. We would mingle in the few remaining wooded acres to savor the changing leaves, and some of us would go as far as walking up either the sandy road or the forest path to get a snippet view of the old beach through the Union Lake Shore's fences running its length; but it was the spirit of those individuals who had lived in the boathouses, along the canal, and in the surrounding forest behind us that had infused the land with their lively energy—an essential component for community. And curiously, after the developer had the new Union Lake Sailing Club built on the old beach close to the end of the canal, nothing else was ever built along it or in the surrounding forest. The once-vibrant sandy road and path meandered through what felt like a wasteland, though visually it hadn't changed.

SOMETHING HAPPENED TO me—and I still don't know what it was—in June of the year the photograph was taken. Spring had been hot, sophomore year had ended, and I had only two commitments for the next two and a half months: to babysit a one-year-old boy four days a week and on some Saturday nights and to end a relationship with a replacement boyfriend, who had been filling in for another whom I loved but had been forbidden to see by my father. I was letting go of an unnamable something else as well, with no desire to be with friends or even call them, and I opted not to explore why. I realized for the first time I was in what was called an in-between time of life; I wanted something more, yet I couldn't consciously state yet what that might be. Nevertheless, I didn't seek to change my state of being either. It felt right to be contained within myself. By July Fourth, the replacement boyfriend had disappeared without any effort on my part.

On those days off from babysitting, I would lie out on a beach towel over our prickly crabgrass backyard, looking up at the clouds and determining what animal shapes they would take, while reading my father's collection of Harold Robbins. He had deemed the pool permanently out of commission due to an irreparable leak.

One very hot late afternoon in mid-July (it was well over ninety degrees), my entire body covered in perspiration, I sat up, looked through the grove and over at Union Lake, and heard the lake say, "Swim." And so I did, twice daily from then on. I went in the morning, before the lifeguards arrived, and then again in the early evening, after they left for the day.

"My, has she gotten quiet," a neighbor from down the street remarked to my mom.

Her response was, "Yes, her mind is elsewhere."

No, I refrained from saying aloud, *my mind is just a few feet from here, through the grove and in the lake.* The lake had finally beckoned me. As the swimming shut down my mind, the water cooled my body and serenity followed. Of course, I did not know back then that this was meditation; I swam because it was all I had.

BAREFOOT, I CROSS through the grove, wearing only a bikini and a beach towel around my neck. I go in waist deep and splash my arms to get used to the cold water. When my body has adjusted, I dive in headfirst and swim straight to the sandbar a quarter way across the lake. After doing laps without counting, I turn my direction ninety degrees and flip over on my back for the dead man's float. My arms move ever so gently, propelling forward and paralleling the man-made beach of misplaced, foreign white sand. When I reach my destination, my arms stop. Each one stretches to its farthest point, keeping me afloat over to where Mrs. Fitch's boathouse had once been.

MANY YEARS HAVE passed since that day with the photograph. I no longer take the photograph out, for fear of exposing the remaining emulsion to ambient light and thus causing the image to dissolve completely. I met the photographer on the sandbar in Union Lake. Having recently returned from the Vietnam War, he had watched me swim laps one evening in August. We fell in love soon after. In late October he took this only proof I was ever at the lake. We did not know it would mark the last Indian summer I would spend there. The next year my boyfriend became my husband, and we went away to college together. I never lived at Union Lake again. When we separated, the photographer kept the transparency and gave me only this print, which has transformed into a decaying relic.

As the print aged, the photographic emulsions began a slow dissolution. Layered one over the other, three separate coatings had created the original image. The cyan layer disappeared first. It had been superimposed over the yellow and magenta layers and had given the edges of the image definition, revealing that the irregular bark lines on the stump where I sat had been those of a maple—one the backhoe left behind. The stump clings to the lake embankment where the man-made beach ends. My long hair parts down the middle, spreading equally around my full, oval face and curving down and over my shoulders, landing at the bend of my elbow, each strand documented in tones ranging from ebony earth to clay. Faint laugh lines show on my face in response to upturned lips. My skin is finally blemish-free, with no aid from make-up for cover-up or enhancement. Sunrays cross over my chest and fall on a braided leather bracelet encircling my left wrist—one my father had made for me.

Next, the yellow emulsion followed the cyan in the graded fade. Yellow gave light and, when combined with cyan, had created another color—green—making the image look like it was from life. This radiance is now gone. The receding magenta layer is all that remains today. So what is left of me is an image in red—not blood red or rose or madder, but a browning red like the fallen leaves around the stump where I had sat. But did the photo have these details when the three emulsions comprised the full color image? Or am I remembering the transparency I saw once or twice, which must have contained them all?

There are days with warm temperatures in late October when the mesmerizing light will seize me for a moment here in my home in Brooklyn, just long enough to recall the photograph taken on another Indian summer day when I was sixteen. The entire roll of film had pleased me. For the first time in a long time, I had accepted an image of the way I looked. In that image I appear to float above the ground on a pedestal. Fallen brown oak, maple, and sassafras leaves, layered in a scallop-feathered pattern, surround the base not yet flattened by rain, footsteps, or impending decay. Frost had begun this weave of foliage two weeks earlier—a weave going from yellow to red and, finally, to brown.

Through my patio door, a golden glow flickers and catches my attention. Refracting sunshine combined with the reflection from the transitory leaves of my willow and ferns and the neighbor's tall birch, hanging over the yellow-painted garden wall, create an aureate dome over the patio. I walk over and cross the threshold into the autumnal light. Warmth instantly embraces me, while my garden's beauty holds me still—no leaves have fallen and all foliage and blossoms remain intact.

PART III

August 27, 2005

I DREAMT LAST night of being in the home where I grew up on Union Lake. Alex parked our Volvo station wagon, a vehicle we didn't own when my mother was alive, in the driveway next to the house. Adriana sat in the back seat. I got out the car and walked over to the side door to enter through the kitchen. The screen door latch clicked free as my thumb pressed the release button, which meant no one was at home; if someone were at home, the latch would have been locked. Once inside, I knew for certain the house was vacant, because the kitchen looked the same as when I had sold it. The table and chairs remained where I had left them, and the appliances were intact. Except for a large picture hook on the blank wall behind the dining table, there seemed to be no sign of the new owner. Alex and Adriana walked behind me.

The last time I had actually been in that house, when awake, was two years before. I had stopped by to give the new owner a bottle of Cabernet Sauvignon as a welcoming gift. I noticed he had placed a large still-life painting of a bowl of apples on the only empty wall in the small kitchen. It was square—three feet by three feet—and took up nearly the entire space. The new owner had been in the floral business, and he also collected and sold oil reproductions of the Dutch masters. I don't remember which master this painting copied, but I liked it. Its large size made the room cozier than when my mother had lived there, though it had cut down on the once prominent, sun-filled luminescence. My mother never would have hung such a large work of art in any part of her cottage, and she would have had a bowl of Red Delicious on the table. Here in the dream, the luminosity returned to the kitchen.

I had had many dreams of my childhood home before selling the house. My mother would sit in her rocking recliner, wearing the pink nightgown she was buried in and smiling beatifically, as if patiently waiting for me. I would remind her she was dead, and she would respond with, "Okay." Even after death my mother required my guidance. These childhood home dreams stopped after I passed ownership onto the florist from Philadelphia—until now.

I wandered into the living room and saw that mother's sofa, recliner, and armchair remained in place. Alex and Adriana agreed nothing had changed since I'd sold the cottage. When I got to the foyer leading to her bedroom, I stopped. The smell of cat urine prevented me from going farther.

January 1, 2008

ALEX DROVE UP to the side of my mother's house. I got out of the car and ran out front on Canal Street. The windows were shut, the sheet curtains drawn, and the side door to the kitchen closed. It looked like no one was at home.

Early morning light tinted all the trees golden, those in the grove, the next-door neighbors' yards, and the woods out back, where spring's presence infused the emerging leaves with that particular transient green. Morning dew clung in large droplets to the crab grass in the front lawn, making it appear greener than it would be in an hour or so when the dew evaporated. Though it was humid, the air was not heavy but buoyant.

I looked back at my mother's closed-up house. Usually it was she who didn't realized she was dead. This time it was me; I expected her to be home. Alex got out of the driver's side of our Ford Escape and Adriana emerged from the back. They walked toward me.

Adriana wore long braids, like she did when she was ten years old, and she barely made it to Alex's shoulder. She hasn't had braids in six or seven years and she's slightly taller than Alex now. And we purchased the Escape last year. This misinformation was too much for me to make sense of. I ran toward them, and we returned to the car.

As Alex turned on the engine, a man came out of my mother's house—the boyfriend of the man who had bought the house from me. He looked many years older since I'd last seen him four years ago, when I had brought the new owner two bottles of biodynamic burgundy as a housewarming present. The boyfriend walked around to my side of the car and leaned into the open window. We nodded to one another.

I told him, "I needed to see some green. I don't get enough of it in Brooklyn."

CARLA PORCH

The Wave

_____

SHELLEY'S MERCEDES SOARS down Brigantine Boulevard and over the bridge into Atlantic City, like a schooner gliding over the sea with the right amount of wind behind its sails. The car knows where to go. Its suspension consumes road bumps before there is any indication the car has gone over a pothole. I have forgotten what it is like to be in a luxury automobile, because my small, four-wheel-drive station wagon keeps me aware of surface imperfections. When Shelley shuts off the ignition, I am numb.

The Wave is so close to Brigantine that it doesn't feel like it's in Atlantic City. However, it is—deep within the Trump Marina Casino, a place I would never think to visit, because I don't gamble, but I have agreed to come here and dance.

"YES, I WILL go to the Wave with you tonight, but only if I can close my eyes for an hour or so," I tell Shelley. She and I lounge side by side in her covered swing out on the deck overlooking Brigantine Bay. I could nap right here, but it's close to ninety degrees. It never just gets hot in South Jersey; it always gets hot and humid, though the sticky heat doesn't deter my daughter, Adriana, from doing multiple cartwheels on the lawn in front of us.

"Do you guys want to go to the beach?" Shelley asks.

"Not now," I reply. "The sun is way too strong. We'll get burned. Let's go after four, when we won't have to wear sunscreen." But really what I want to do now is to get back to reading Virginia Woolf's _To the Lighthouse_.

I look out to the sea grasses and cattails receding into the bay. They stand straight up and point to two cirrus bands crisscrossing effortlessly in an otherwise empty, but mesmerizing, deep blue sky. There is no breeze or ozone smog, despite the muggy heat. I tell Shelley I'll see her in a bit. She lights up a cigarette and says she'll stay outside in the swing; her cell phone rings.

Adriana follows me inside. She grabs *The Hitchhikers Guide to the Galaxy*—the last of her required summer reading—from the coffee table and sprawls out on the crescent-shaped sofa in the living room.

"Yeah, only two chapters left," she says, and adds, "I don't get what all the big deal is about this book," as I walk off to Shelley's combination office and spare bedroom.

LAST NIGHT, AT home in Brooklyn, I left Mrs. Ramsay, the central character in *To The Lighthouse*, asking herself as she sits down at the helm of a dining table, "But what have I done with my life?" She and Mr. Ramsay are hosting a dinner party in a rented beach house on the Scottish coast near Edinburgh. The room is sparsely adorned: a table and chairs, platters of food, an arrangement of fruit, table settings, and the diners. To Mrs. Ramsay's left is a row of exposed windows, looking out to a lonely lighthouse beacon and the dark sea beyond. The beacon is her focal point as the diners take their seats. She prefers to have all the guests sit down together while the food is warm. Only the reader knows how much this means to her. Her agitation dissipates with the arrival of four hitherto missing guests. The circle is complete; togetherness flows smoothly among the diners as Mrs. Ramsay breathes in the wholeness of her dinner party. Only for this moment, she no longer struggles with wanting life to be different from what it is right now; her mission for this day has been achieved.

I begin to feel sleepy and decide to stop reading. The first section, "The Window," is near its end. I skim a few passages ahead in the following section, "Time Passes," and the concluding one, "The Lighthouse." Mrs. Ramsay is referred to in the distant past; she must have died. How can the story continue without her? Her physical beauty and life force provide the story's vitality. I too have fallen under the spell of her charisma. Mrs. Ramsay signifies the quintessential mother—one who cherishes her offspring's childhood and believes it to be necessary to experience childhood to the fullest. She sees her solitary houseguests not living life to the fullest because of their incapacity to share their lives with others; whereas, for her, there is no other way to be. Mrs. Ramsay's compassion for their aloneness compels her to alleviate what she perceives as their loneliness, if only during their stay with her and her family on the Scottish coast.

However, Mrs. Ramsay is a contradiction—a quality that has made me her ally. Before the dinner party, she sits alone and gazes at the lighthouse beacon while knitting a wool sock for the lighthouse keeper's son. She lets the preparations for the dinner party, what the children are up to, and the contentment of her houseguests recede from the forefront of her thoughts. "For now she need not think about anybody. She could be herself, by herself ... To be silent; to be alone ... When life sank down for a moment, the range of experience seemed limitless."[3]

Mr. Ramsay walks by and wants to approach her. "She was lovely, lovelier now than ever he thought ... But he resolved, no; he would not interrupt her ... though it hurt him that she should look so distant, and he could not reach her ..."[4]

In disappointment, I put *To the Lighthouse* next to me on the bed; I shouldn't have looked ahead. I close my eyes, transfer the traffic sounds along Brigantine Boulevard into the waves crashing on their shore, and begin drowsily scanning in my mind the clothes I have brought that would work at the Wave. I choose the red, pink, and yellow rose-print skirt with the mauve tank top, and over that the pale pink cardigan. Though it is hot now, the wind will pick up later at night on the Atlantic City Harbor when I'm walking over to the Wave. Besides, the tank top may show too much of my breasts, and if I feel out of my element, I can cover them. For my feet, the hot pink, pointy slip-ons feel the most comfortable for dancing, and they complement the skirt.

The familiar naughty sensation I get when I go out with Shelley returns. This is a conditioned response, since I have no one to answer to anymore. My father is deceased; my mother wishes she too could go dancing if she were able; my husband knows I plan to go out with Shelley; and my daughter is old enough to stay alone for a few hours by herself at night.

Shelley and I have been buddies for nearly forty years, since elementary school. We began our escapades by cutting Sunday school in sixth grade. I can't remember what we did or where we went for that one hour. There wasn't much trouble we could get into at eleven o'clock on a Sunday morning, but it was the freedom from Methodist ideology that bonded us.

Our adventures escalated until our sophomore year. I realized then that I wanted to go to college and became serious about academics. Shelley got a secretarial job working for Prudential Insurance even before she was graduated from high school and continued working there for the next twenty years. Afterward, she retired to become a real estate broker, divorced her husband, and moved to Brigantine so she could live at the shore—she had always wanted to live near the ocean. The last time the two of us went out dancing, she was still with Husband Number Two.

I wake up from the nap, not knowing where I am, as if coming out of anesthesia, until I hear a car honking outside and realize I am at Shelley's in Brigantine. I stir slowly, beginning with my fingers and toes. Then I get up, go over to the suitcase, and take out a bikini and the outfit I will be wearing later.

IT'S PAST FOUR o'clock. Adriana and I are ready for a swim in the ocean. This will no doubt be our last time in the Atlantic until next year, since it is the weekend before Labor Day. We like walking to the beach, but Shelley insists on driving us; her cottage is bayside, four blocks from the ocean.

When we arrive at the beach, Adriana runs to the edge of the water and yells to me, "I'll go in tomorrow. It's too cold."

I rush over to check. She's right; the ocean does feel cold, almost too cold to go in, though the air temperature is still in the mideighties.

"We won't have time tomorrow. We have to get back to Brooklyn. Come on, you're tough," I respond. My determination drives me to get in that final swim of the season, no matter what.

Adriana's sensitivity to cold has increased over the past year. Until she was twelve, she paid little attention to water temperature, whether it was in the ocean, lake, river, or swimming pool. She would dive in and then would have to be begged to "please come out."

Once she stayed in a swimming pool all day, doing handstands and rollovers. When she finally emerged from the water, she looked reptilian.

Her lips had become aubergine and the whites of her eyes pomegranate, intensifying the green of her irises to mimic faceted emeralds. She spoke quickly, because she had been submerged so long and hadn't said a word in all those hours. "Did you see how long I stayed under holding my handstand, Mommy?" In those days, she prefaced every sentence with "Did you see …?"

Now she hesitates and whines, "Mom, it's too cold."

I'm not pleased with the temperature either but keep the discomfort to myself and proceed into deeper waters. Adriana follows closely behind me.

The rough late-August waves come in at various angles, making it hard to gauge when to dive under or to jump through and making it impossible for either of us to swim a standard crawl. With each break, the strong undertow drags us ever so slightly south toward Atlantic City. We are good swimmers, but there are few others in the water, and these conditions make me nervous.

A large wave angling from the southeast snags Adriana. She surrenders, letting it drag her down, but she dives under the next one from due east and comes up through the ten-second calm before the next mélange of waves breaks and rolls toward us.

"Come on, Mommy, don't be such a baby," she cries before she ducks the next convergence. I haven't yet submerged my head, because I can't get my footing in this turbulence. She does a dolphin kick toward me through the next calm as I dive below the breaking wave to my right and swim underwater toward her.

Shelley sits on a large towel to the right of the lifeguard's chair. She holds a cigarette in her left hand as her right turns a radio dial. In my haste to get into the ocean, I had not noticed the radio when we laid down our towels and kicked off our flip-flops. Why would she want to listen to a radio here and not intermingle with this environment? The wind from the south moves sculpted cumulus clouds over the ocean as cirrus strips above the bay emulate peach-colored ribbons floating in front of the setting golden sun. Sharp light shafts etch along the dunes while lanky beach grasses sway back and forth like a choir of gospel singers. Waves crash on the shore in dissonance. Shelley seems one step removed, observing all of this as if it were on a large, flat television screen.

"Why don't you have your suit on?" I'd asked back at her cottage.

She replied that she just wanted to sit at the shore. I knew she doesn't like to get her hair wet, so I pushed further.

"The ocean does all the work. All you have to do is jump up to the oncoming wave so it doesn't crash into your face. And salt water is good for you." My final plea was, "The summer's nearly over, and it's hurricane season. The undertow is getting stronger, and riptides appear without notice. The lifeguards leave the day after Labor Day, and it could be too dangerous to go in without them. By then, the water gets too cold to swim."

She had been crying before we had arrived earlier that morning, greeting us with a blotchy red face. Her reason was that a coworker at her real estate office had died suddenly yesterday from a heart attack, soon after leaving work. She had been working with him on a project just an hour before his death. I heard myself speaking words of comfort, attempting to allay her pain, but what I saw was my oldest friend, frail and aging beyond her time. I sensed that her pain ran deeper than the loss of this coworker.

I bob my head up and see the lifeguards dragging the rescue boat from the shoreline over toward their tall chair—a signal that their workday will end soon. I estimate we've been dodging the waves for over thirty minutes when Adriana's head hits the back of my knees. I open them so she can swim through, and then I dive behind her, just missing being cast aside by a large wave coming in on a diagonal. I grab her backside and tickle her waist.

Our heads bob up for air in unison, and I say in a gulping yell, "We should go in now."

Her response is, "No, Mommy. Five more minutes."

Down we dive, holding hands, resting for seconds on the ocean floor as cascades blend together over our heads.

ADRIANA LOUNGES ON the crescent sofa in front of Shelley's wide-screen television and flips through many channels; we don't have cable at home.

I place a kiss on my daughter's forehead and tell her to please behave while I'm out with Shelley, adding, "We won't be gone long."

Adriana's plan is to watch *Dogma*, a film about two fallen angels. Shelley took her to the video store while I napped and let her pick whatever she wanted. I had seen *Dogma* when it first came out and left the theater feeling I had wasted my time because I was disappointed with the director, Kevin Smith; I had loved his previous film, *Chasing Amy*.

"How can it be all that bad, Mom? It has Matt Damon and Ben Affleck as the angels," Adriana said. She knows how I despise bad cinema, but I surrender her, this time, to mediocrity.

Shelley comes into the living room, wearing black capris and a white spaghetti-strap tank top. She explains to Adriana that if she needs to reach an adult while we're gone, she can go over to the landlord, who lives next door.

While Shelley is speaking, I look down at my outfit and see a rhapsody of pink. Maybe this is too much pink? But what can I change into? This is the only outfit I have with me that I could wear to a nightclub. I've worn it in New York City, upstate, Cape Cod, and throughout Florida. We don't have to be the Bobbsey Twins, like we were sometimes in junior high. I'm not changing.

Repeating to Adriana, "I'll be back soon," and then adding, "I love you," I relinquish her to *Dogma*.

Shelley offers to drive, and in unison, we slide into her Mercedes' oversized seats and pull the seat belts across our bodies.

SHELLEY HAS LEFT me alone at the bar while she dances with one of her Wave buddies, a man named Jacques. He had strolled over minutes before from the slot machines outside the club entrance. She and I were sitting on the only two available seats, center position, along a horseshoe-shaped bar.

His first statement, directed to me before Shelley could introduce us, was, "What's wrong with her hair?" Windswept wisps had fallen out of Shelley's French twist and surrounded her face. The breeze off Atlantic City harbor had been brisk as she and I watched the egg-shaped moon rising from the marina before we entered the casino. Yes, Shelley was windswept, but she looked fresh and exhilarated.

"I am from Europe, where women are groomed," Jacques proclaimed.

Shelley looked at me, while repeating several times, "What's wrong with my hair?"

"Nothing," I said, shaking my head every time she asked.

My hand touched my hair falling over my shoulders, and I felt ripples. *How does Jacques see my hair?* I thought to myself. *It must be in layered tentacles going in all directions, which is how it behaves when I am by the sea.*

The dance music, incessant repetitive beats generated by a computer, began as Jacques lifted up his left eyebrow and opened his hands toward me.

My head shook back and forth as my mouth said, "No, thank you, Jacques." He turned away from me and grabbed Shelley's hands, and off they went to the dance floor, leaving me alone at the bar.

MRS. RAMSAY, I am here at the Wave, sitting in the center of a horseshoe-shaped bar, equidistant from its end points, drinking a white wine spritzer, and talking with a man named Gary. He looks Italian, my height, a bit chubby, and seems at least ten years younger than me. He tells me he was a quarterback at Temple University fifteen years ago. Directly opposite from where I sit, the television broadcasts the Philadelphia Eagles playing a preseason game against Tampa Bay. I hate football, but I can't escape it.

Gary is with a blonde woman, approximately his age, who is sitting on his other side. He doesn't include her in our conversation, nor does she attempt to join in. While he recounts his college football career to me, Gary says, in an aside, that he and the woman are just friends. He doesn't use her proper name, only "she."

"We come here together because I'm friendly and know how to get her guys," he boasts.

Can Gary see me shudder, Mrs. Ramsay?

Tampa Bay scores a touchdown, and the entire bar boos. The Eagles are the local team; Philadelphia is sixty miles due west. When the booing subsides, Gary introduces me to a man who has leaned between us to order a drink. He looks fifteen years older than I do; he is baldheaded with bits of gray hair lying on either side and has a large potbelly. The man signals to the bartender to give me another drink. With my index finger and thumb, I signal back just a bit of Chardonnay.

"Where do you come from?" the man inquires. He works for Verizon on Fourth Avenue in Brooklyn.

Oh God, Mrs. Ramsay, how do I get out of this? I live three blocks from there.

Shelley returns with Jacques. My head turns away from the Verizon man, and I mouth "Help" in her direction. She laughs at me with her eyes and then directs them toward the man. Another man, with hair styled in what my mother calls a pompadour, emerges from behind Shelley. I shudder again.

She grabs his arm and says, "Hi, Don. Here's my friend Carla from New York. Dance with her."

My mouth says, "Hello, Don," but my voice elicits, "Sorry, Don. I am not ready."

No, I am not ready to dance. A magnetic force keeps my bottom glued to the barstool and both of my legs wrap-locked around its pedestal. My ethereal self does not want to move onto the dance floor, and neither does my body. This is so unlike me.

Every blow-dried strand on Don's head is in place, from forehead to crown, creating a wide tiara of hair. I can't possibly dance with a man who looks like that. A giggle, which I convert into a little dry cough, wells up from my throat, and I cover my mouth with my hand. He looks like a nice man, with his creased gray slacks and short-sleeved, pale blue, tucked-in oxford shirt. His feet are encased in brown Italian leather loafers with tassels, and there's a whiff of aftershave—an old scent I recognize, like Hai Karate. But it's his hair.

"You go ahead, Shelley."

Where's my compassion, Mrs. Ramsay, my acceptance of others as they are?

My gaze returns to the television, where Tampa Bay is close to making another touchdown. I veer to the right, and the man from Verizon is gone.

"He wasn't your type?" Gary inquires.

Shaking my head and exhaling through my nostrils, I say, "No. No, he wasn't."

Gary's nameless, nearly faceless blonde friend talks to a new man at the bar. She has become animated. Her nose comes to a pleasing point, and her thin lips mouth words. Her sea-blue eyes dart back and forth, and she smiles while speaking, the corners of her lips forming a slight, upward crinkle at the ends. Between where she is standing and the oppressive beat from the dance floor, I can't make out what she is saying to the new man.

Gary pulls me over, cups my right ear, and says, "I think that guy's gay. Don't you?"

Right now, Mrs. Ramsay, I will use any diversion, so I don't have to watch a football game or feel compelled to dance with a middle-aged man with a blow-dried pompadour.

"Do I think he's gay?" I ask. The new man and I lock gazes.

"He's gay, right?" Gary insists in my ear.

"No, he's not," I reply.

I had eye contact like this with an owl in central Vermont earlier this summer. I had one hour to go for a hike while Adriana took a horseback-riding lesson. My arms pumped quickly back and forth as my hiking boots gripped the gravelly ascent beyond the riding stables, cutting through green pastures on either side. I then descended into a dense hemlock forest by climbing over sporadically placed granite boulders. The temperature went from pasture-warm dry to forest-damp cool, sharpening my focus. A crow squawked, a bobwhite whistled, and then silence, except for my hiking boots sliding on rocks. The damp atmosphere encouraged a somewhat honeysuckle, somewhat earth smell, but its detection was hard for my nose to hold. I kept breathing deeply to figure out what it was, so I could remember later.

I looked down at my wristwatch and saw that I had walked for thirty minutes; Adriana's lesson was halfway over. Turning around to ascend the hill back, I faced a white snowy owl perched on a long hemlock branch a few arm lengths away. Her green eyes latched onto my brown ones, and our gazes fixed to each other; we exchanged a timeless contact. My hands felt as if they were on either side of her face, although I knew my body had not left where I stood. The next moment, I was running up the hill and back to the stable.

The new man breaks his gaze to nod to the blonde woman, whose face has returned to its expressionless state.

She pulls Gary's arm and he leans over and says in my ear, "I got to go. She's bugging me."

Gary disappears with the now nearly featureless woman among the slot machines beyond the entrance.

The new man moves next to me, where Gary had been sitting, and asks, "How long have you been a friend of Shelley's?"

"How do you know I'm a friend of Shelley's?"

"You were talking to her before she went off to dance with Don. I saw you mouth 'Help,' and your eyes looked like they were pleading to get away from here."

"You saw all of that? When?" I ask.

"You didn't see me pass behind you just a while ago, when the older guy bought you the drink?"

"No, I didn't. Yes, I'm Shelley's friend. We've been friends since we were ten."

"Oh, how rare to be friends for so long."

Shelley returns to the bar with Don and says, "Hi, Rick," to the new man.

"Hey, Shelley."

"Hey, Rick, dance with my friend Carla," Shelley says.

"No, I'm still not ready yet," I say.

"Then dance with me, Rick."

"Okay, Shelley." Rick grabs her hand, and they dissolve into the bopping crowd.

Relief, Mrs. Ramsay, has been bestowed upon me, again.

But why is it that I cannot detach my ass from the seat? The white wine spritzer tastes like bile now.

"What happened?" I ask the drink. "You were thirst-quenching earlier." I shove the remaining drink to the edge of the bar and fold my hands so the back of my thumbs touch and place them palms up in my lap. My head turns and I scan the horseshoe bar.

Not one woman is dressed like me; nobody is in pink. All are in white or black spaghetti-strap tank tops, with converging mountainous breasts meeting at fault-line cleavages. Bottom halves have been poured into tight, hip-hugger blue jeans or black capris, and long hairdos are held in place with either gel or mousse. While heads sway and lips pucker at preening suitors, undulating strands of hair stay as a unified mass, so no loose ends.

My eyes travel down to my folded hands as two long, soft curls fall forward. Each hits the side of my nose and curls in at my nostril. My hands lie in a field of pink, red, and yellow rosebuds. My eyes move upward from my lap to the pale pink cardigan—the protective membrane concealing the clinging mauve tank holding my breasts in mounds with a shallow valley between. My chest rises as breath moves from my nose and goes down to my belly.

Again, I gaze over at the row of Medusa-headed mannequins and their undifferentiated breasts around the bar.

"My God, all of them are fake," I say with an exhale.

The disco light swirls around and shines over to the bar from the dance floor, blinking slowly and out of sync with the computer-generated thumping which has become louder and more like a heart beating on "reverb." Strobes fall askew on grinning, gaping faces; harsh glare transforms skin tones into deadly white—momentary rigor mortis. These gloating, freeze-dried masks are like those street revels I remember from *Black Orpheus,* when Eurydice is running frantically through Rio de Janeiro's far-reaching carnival parade, crying out to Orpheus to save her from Death. The phantom revelers, like those around me, were oblivious to her distress with their swirling, ecstatic, samba parading, slowing her in her flight.

Rick's voice enters my left ear: "Are you okay?"

Startled, I say, "Did you ever see *Black Orpheus,* Rick?"

"What's that? A movie?" Rick asks. He sits on the edge of his stool with his elbow on the bar ledge.

"Yes, it's a film from Brazil, based on the Greek myth of Orpheus, the harp player, and Eurydice, his wife. When Orpheus played his harp, he made the sun rise. Eurydice journeys into the underworld in an unsuccessful attempt to flee from Death. After retrieving Eurydice's body, Orpheus looks back from where he came in the underworld. Because he looks back, Death not only catches up with Eurydice but with Orpheus as well. *Black Orpheus* is set in Rio de Janeiro during carnival."

Rick turns his body to face mine.

Mrs. Ramsay, does this mean he's interested in what I am saying?

I move in closer and begin: "A beautiful young woman stands at the helm of a passenger ferry as it enters the harbor in Rio ..."

The Elevator

A MAN LEADS me into an empty elevator. Once we are inside, his left pointer finger pushes the button to the fourteenth floor. My eyes survey the surroundings as the door closes. Overhead the fluorescent light glows ochre, neutralizing the silvery, cool walls covered in stainless steel panels from floor to ceiling. My attention then turns to the man. No joke—he is tall, dark, and handsome.

He gazes straight ahead and takes his left hand and lays it over his right, resting them on his lower abdomen. I move closer to him, arms side by side, and my height reaches to his shoulder. Neither of us speaks. The elevator kicks in and ascends in near silence—no grinding gears or even a fluorescent hum; I hear only a soft drone from rising. Then, a slight whistling sound comes out of my nose as I exhale. Can the man hear that? This is not the kind of attention I want drawn to myself. Could he be thinking, I'm bringing her to my home, and the first thing I learn about her is that she has a cold? I look up at him apologetically, and he smiles sweetly back at me.

A warm jolt from inside me shoots out of my eyes and down my throat, spreading throughout my chest. Pathways down my arms carry it to my fingertips, causing them to tingle. What energy remains splits again, shooting out of the base of my torso and down my legs, while the soles of my feet hold fast to the steel floor.

Time has slowed down, and the elevator ride takes longer than usual. The lighted dial above the door shows seven floors still to go. My right arm goes under the man's left elbow. My hand slides slowly down his jacket sleeve, savoring its mohair softness. When I reach the cuff, the tingling in my fingertips stops. My eyes focus on the man's hands: rows of fine, black hairs and raised veins cover olive skin, hinting of male strength.

The elevator stops with a double thump, but the doors open with barely a sound.

"We're here," the man says softly, and he holds the door with his free arm. I release my hand from his left cuff, taking in the mohair softness from reverse, and cross the threshold into the fourteenth-floor hallway.

Coração

MY LEFT HAND goes through the bend of a man's right arm and rests on the sleeve of his jacket. I wear a red hibiscus-print sundress and a large-brimmed straw hat; he is in a khaki-colored linen suit and has no hat. We stand side by side, facing a tall counter. My hand squeezes his jacket sleeve hard enough for me to feel his taut forearm; his free hand taps the bell on top of the counter.

Brilliant white light comes through a large bay window off to the side, falling on a smattering of scallop shells attached to a jute fish net hanging from a wall of driftwood paneling behind the tall counter. At once I feel familiarity with this light and at ease in this setting. An older man, dressed in a black two-piece suit and black tie—perhaps the concierge—appears from behind the counter. I ask him if there is a cheap motel outside of town. He opens a map and lays it out in front of my companion and me. I recognize the land formation; we are on the Delmarva Peninsula, below Ocean City, Maryland, and closer to the Atlantic Ocean than to the Chesapeake Bay. As the concierge's finger traces the route to the cheap motel, he tells us, in an ever-so-slight Southern accent, when leaving here we must turn left and then right at the ocean.

My traveling companion and I lie in the center of a king-size bed and caress each other's naked bodies. The oversized bed nearly fills the dark, dingy-colored room, leaving no walking space. We must be at the cheap motel. This body I caress feels like my husband's, although he has appeared in the doorway of the empty closet, fully dressed, across from my side of the bed, yelling at me, "What suitcase do I need?"

As I am about to respond to him, the refrain from a samba, "Samba da Benção," begins playing in my head, but I hear only one of its lyrics:

"coração." He stares at me with frightened eyes, asking repeatedly which suitcase he needs. The one-lyric samba plays so loudly over his voice that I can see only his mouth moving.

I call back to him with a single word: "Cortisone"—the anti-inflammatory medication.

AFTER TAKING TWO days to file last year's income taxes, a task I thought was only going to take two hours, I reward myself with a late morning cross-country ski on new-fallen snow in Prospect Park's Long Meadow.

While getting the gear ready, I feel feverish and think, *Oh, it's just my cold or my period,* (since I have both) but I take my temperature anyway. It's 97.4 degrees. I need to get out and raise my metabolism.

It's in the midforties outside, so skiing on a warm winter morning such as this has an upside and a downside. The upside is the exhilaration I'll feel, because I love heat and love to ski with a minimal amount of outerwear: a shell covering a cotton turtleneck and no thermals under my ski pants will suffice. The downside is that fallen snow at this temperature melts before one's eyes. The parallel trails I'll create in the snow with my skis will instantly become grassy in my wake.

Upon entering Long Meadow, I place my much-loved Alpina cross-country skis down and snap into the bindings. Knowing how responsive these skis are, I feel competent when I glide and do the skating technique. I pick up my thigh and move it forward. The real workout will be in my buttocks. Despite the mélange of paw and footprints imbedded into last night's snowfall, plenty of virgin, powdery snow has survived for me to make clean trails.

Up and down I go on Long Meadow's hills, which are actually mounds ten to twenty feet high. Though small in size, the mounds present a challenge today, since their sides are covered in watery ice sheets. The herringbone technique is the only way up. At the base, I place the skis at a forty-five-degree angle to each other and proceed by picking up my left leg and then my right as fast as I can, carving a herringbone pattern into melting ice behind me. After mounting the highest hill, I turn around with much trepidation, and instantly I am back at the bottom, standing in a perfect stop position. Up and down I go—agile and never falling, and always landing with perfection. Thank you, Alpina.

Before making the final descent from a mound covered with oak and plane trees, I look up at open sky. My tinted sunglasses give it a Maxfield Parrish look: a sea-green sky overlaid with white cumulus clouds outlined in rose-rouge gray. My eyes fill with awe as I gaze at this wondrous sight, and my heart swells—or maybe my rising body temperature has created this sentiment within me.

I return home exhausted, turn on the CD player, and take a shower. The seductive afternoon glow of my bedroom, derived from the reflected yellow garden walls onto the peach-colored ones here inside, draws me to lie down and savor my exertion. With the volume set barely to audible, I recognize the music playing; it is "Samba da Benção." The samba soothes me to sleep. I sleep maybe five minutes and wake up to another samba. It's not the change of music that brings me consciousness but the word coração, the one word in "Samba da Benção" that I understand—the Portuguese word for heart.

THE BALMY AIR hints of impending spring, though it's early March, and the waxing, egg-shaped moon, beaming down on my left side, accompanies me as I stroll home through Park Slope. The lyric "coração" along with a riff from a sax from "Samba da Benção" plays in my head. I have now translated coração into corazón, the word for heart in Spanish, a language of which I have some comprehension.

I open the door to my apartment and look over at the clock above the kitchen stove. It says it is 11:00 p.m. My daughter is already asleep, since it is a school night for her, and my husband is probably asleep as well. Whenever I get home late at night and the others are asleep, a sense of loneliness passes through me. I become awakened by walking at night, and I have an intense desire to share my experience, but there is no one to share it with. However, this time I see the rose quartz nightlight is on in my bedroom—a beacon that indicates my husband may still be awake.

My husband lies on my side of our bed and says, "Come here; let's park"—our words for cuddle. I get ready for bed quickly.

As I slide into bed with him, I ask, "How was your healing circle?" He replies the circle tonight had worked with a man who has been diagnosed by his doctor as a schizophrenic, but actually he is just plain lonely.

Sleep begins to overtake me. My last words to my husband are to tell him that we need a honeymoon, while in my head the last word I hear is corazón.

I DREAM I am in bed, naked in the arms of another man who is not my husband, in a cramped motel room. It's too spare to be anything else. To my left, my husband stands in a closet next to a stack of suitcases. He is asking me which suitcase belongs to him. My daughter sits by the foot of the bed at a small, white card table, laying out those advertising postcards she always picks up from the back of restaurants in a tarot format.

She looks up at me with her large, sober green eyes and says, "Pick, Mommy."

I respond, "Coração."

Air-Dried

I HEAR THE neighbor's clothesline pulley screeching outside as I walk through my front door. Has it ever been this loud or shrill before? I place the bag of groceries on the floor and go over to the open patio door to peer above the trees in my garden and across the courtyard. Various colored items, each grouped together by category—washcloths, bath and hand towels, and pillowcases—have been pinned to the line and flap like Tibetan prayer flags in the breeze. A gust then thrusts the pillowcases above the fire escape window, revealing the laundress climbing back into her home.

Hanging clothes outside is not something I would do here in Brooklyn. Traffic-generated dust is perennially in the air, caused by the double lanes of traffic just a few feet from my garden on Fourth Avenue. And the only place where I can smell fresh air is in the center of Prospect Park, several blocks up the street, but it's not sweet in the way air can be. Maybe the mysterious laundress, a portion of whose fluttering skirt is all I ever see when she stands on the fire escape balcony, has no other means to dry her wet laundry, or she's determined to line dry rather than use a dryer, despite the dusty sprinklings. We live too far away from each other for me to call out to her across the courtyard with my queries.

My mood has been heavy with a new kind of sadness these past few days, because my mother's birthday is approaching. When I closed the sale of her house on that date, I took it as a good sign, because I was being released from a long, distant burden on the day of her birth. As I watch the wash blowing in the wind now across the courtyard, I realize today marks three years since the last time I hung laundry on her clothesline—a thought I had not had until now.

On the final day of emptying my mother's house of all her possessions and cleaning it for the next owner, I washed the linen I wanted to keep and hung it out on the clothesline in the backyard. I had even brought my dirty laundry from Brooklyn. That August day was perfect for drying: mideighties, no clouds, and low humidity. Every so often I glanced up at the sky—such a deep blue for a South Jersey dog day. The fresh air was what I loved about the place; its sweetness, I knew, would embed itself into the weave of the fabric as it blew whatever it was I hung to dry.

I pinned up the first load at eight in the morning and finished four rounds later by four o'clock in the afternoon, and then I locked the door forever with my mother's key.

"You've got your own life in New York," my mother would say, no matter what borough I was living in or during my two-year stay in eastern Long Island. Even though she knew I would never keep her house after she died, her voice would then rise slightly and become a bit softer: "You could keep it to come down on weekends." The house was a two-and-a-half-hour drive from Brooklyn. My father had built it on Union Lake in southern New Jersey, and she had lived there for nearly sixty years. Nine months after her death, I sold her home to a florist in Philadelphia who planned to retire soon. Philadelphia was not the place where he wanted to grow old. He yearned to return to where he had grown up; he wanted to grow old on Union Lake.

I couldn't go back to where I had grown up, not even for weekends. Too many things had changed, particularly the lake community, and just a few of my other relatives remained in the area. The only draw for the last several years had been seeing my mother, and without her there, I had no desire to be in the house. I sold it without regrets, or so I thought.

My mother had been an artist at line drying. As soon as I had grown too big for the swing set located in the center of our backyard, she convinced my father to create an open square clothesline system in its place. He was reluctant at first, because he had become somewhat lazy in his middle age. However, he knew how tired she was of the row-upon-row, cotton-line arrangement off to one side of the yard, which she claimed slowed down drying and made more work for her. "It's hard for the air to go through the wash," she argued. She also wanted the wash to hang from a plastic-coated clothesline, so she could wipe off the accumulated grime before the first hanging. Our clothes always had short, gray indented marks where the pins had attached the laundry to the cotton clothesline, and she hated that. But more importantly, my mother was ready for expansion. She wanted her clothes to dry faster so that she could do more than one load on a dry, sunny day. Her concluding argument was, "I could finally keep up with the wash"—a Sisyphean challenge for a laundress without a dryer.

So as the neighbors from two doors down carried away my old swing set for their two younger children, my father with his pole digger began digging in the northeast corner of our yard. The new system would consist of four poles, each sunk into the ground and cemented into place. My mother held the pole upright while my father poured concrete. After the cement hardened, my father strung a plastic-coated clothesline from pole to pole at the top, and then he secured each juncture with a boating knot. The clothesline was ready for the following morning's wash—strung taut, like violin string, and creating a perfect overhead square.

No longer would there be the need for propping sticks, an essential with the cotton line, particularly to prevent a full-size wet sheet from dragging on the sandy ground. Nor would my mother be running outside every time one of the sticks fell down. And there would be no more dried-in gray marks marring our clothes. The backyard was now her drying quarter, a room open to the sky. Meticulously, she hung items by category: paired socks, bath towels, my dad's white T-shirts, and his long-legged work pants. She transformed a situation that wasn't working for her to one that did.

Sometimes on hot days, when I still ran wild for no apparent reason, I would duck under archways fashioned from side-by-side hand towels, my father's jockey shorts, and my mother's bras and slips, or between a wall of bed linens the wind picked up, and enter her magical space. Those warm breezes blowing through the wet laundry transformed the balmy, open square into a cool humidity while holding me in the center as I spun circles, looking up at the sky.

AFTER DOWNLOADING GOOGLE Earth, I type in the address of my mother's house. Within seconds the satellite image zooms down from the entire Western Hemisphere to the Mid-Atlantic States to southern New Jersey and Union Lake. For an instant the entire image is just Union Lake. The cursor moves to the right and stops on the correct street. It is not directly on where my mother's house was located but rather in front of the first house at the beginning of the block. I move the cursor down five houses, and the drying quarter appears.

The trees are bare; no looming shadows from foliage shade the backyard. Two white, square items, perhaps sheets, hang from the line closest to the house.

Epilogue

The First Encounter

WE RUSHED ACROSS the parking lot and leaned the bikes against the guard railing at First Encounter Beach. We had made it in time: the sun had not set yet. It was still complete and rested just above the point where turquoise, red, and orange sky met shadowy bay. No clouds were in sight. The evening air idled, holding onto its late afternoon warmth; it was still too balmy to wear the sweatshirts tied to our waists. My husband, daughter, and I stood transfixed, watching the sun descend. Where we live in Brooklyn, sunsets are blocked by rows of brownstones that, from any vantage point, obstruct our view of the west. It would be some time before we would get a chance to see another sunset like this. What a send-off!

Dusk quickly approached. We got back on the bikes in reluctant silence, knowing we should return to the rental cottage before dark, since the bikes only had reflectors and the roads back had no shoulder. Besides, we needed to begin packing if we wanted to get in a final swim before leaving in the morning. Before pedaling off, we turned around to give the setting sun a last look, when we noticed a glint from the diminishing light fell on a brass plaque perched on the beach, close to where we stood straddling the bikes. We had rented the same cottage by this beach for the past several summers and never noticed the plaque.

My daughter read the inscription aloud. It stated the Mayflower Company had trespassed on the Nauset people's land, a surprising discovery as this was the only acknowledgment of the Indian people's dispossession we had ever seen anywhere on Cape Cod. Had it been placed here during the previous year? No, it had been put here in 2001—a year we hadn't come to the Cape.

I glanced over at my husband and saw his face soften. He is from Peru and indigenous on his mother's side, a fact he had recognized only in the past ten years. Prior to that, he had felt compelled to exist in the amorphous identity of a mestizo. Though more aboriginal in appearance, he had identified closely with being white.

He looked back at me and said, in his half-serious, half-joking manner, "Finally, some of your people want to set history straight."

I vowed to return at sunrise and take a shot of this commemoration. Since the plaque faced directly east, the sun would shine on it at a low angle at that hour and illuminate the raised letters with just the right amount of light, avoiding an overexposure. And perhaps it would provide a turning point to what was becoming a collection of the rather standard beach vacation photographs I had shot so far.

At dawn of the following day, I took off alone for First Encounter Beach. Plumes from the swaying marsh grasses ahead shimmered with early morning light, mesmerizing me. I came back from my momentary revelry to realize I might have already missed sunrise. My hands clutched the brakes in time for the bicycle to make a smooth, sharp right onto Samoset Road. With less than a mile to go, I pedaled fast, so fast my French braid thumped my back like a riding crop, and both halves of my long wraparound skirt flapped behind me like a power sail. At the end of Samoset, I slowed down to pass through the unmanned attendant's gate leading into First Encounter Beach. The skirt halves swooped under my backside and over my thighs, remaining in place as I bee-lined across the empty parking lot. The beach was silent, except for the screech from the hand brakes.

Light loomed only from the far side of the sand dunes at the end of the parking lot. The rising sun had not yet reached the embossed letters on the plaque, and I knew if I took a shot of it then, it would come out underexposed. I dismounted, parked my bike at the edge of the pavement, and walked a few feet onto the beach to wait for the anticipated effect I wanted. Aside from the footprints stretching out behind me, there were no others on the beach.

At first glance the bay appeared to be still, and then my eyes could make out rippling, minuscule waves rolling in, while sandpipers, sea kites, and gulls waded in swirl-shaped tidal pools at the water's edge. Two electric-blue dragonflies appeared, the size of hummingbirds, and flew in concentric circles above my head. A warm, gentle breeze surrounded my body and held me at a standstill, infusing the wisps held tight in my braid to release and caress the sides of my face. I let myself linger with this bittersweet feeling of oneness. Closing my eyes, I heard the soft, white noise of the tide's return, joined by a bay gull's squawk sharpening the stillness. Dawn's clarity prevailed.

An engine roared behind me and then shut off. Doors released and slammed. I walked back to the now sun-gilded inscription and quickly pulled out the Leica from my backpack. As the couple from the SUV walked out of camera range, I lifted the camera above the plaque and adjusted the zoom lens from close-up to wide angle. Through the viewfinder, I saw radiance spread above the plaque and across the width of the bay; golden sandbars striped the blue water, holding fast despite the tide's rush to shore—contrasts now heightened between sky, sea, and beach. Within an hour, the water would be high enough to swim a lap spanning from one end of First Encounter Beach to the other, my final one for this summer. I resumed taking several more exposures.

THIS TEXT INSCRIBED on the brass plaque at First Encounter Beach in Eastham, Massachusetts, said:

> Near this site the Nauset Tribe of the Wampanoag Nation seeking to protect themselves and their culture had their First Encounter, December 8, 1620, with Myles Standish, John Carver, William Bradford, Edward Winslow, John Tilley, Edward Tilley, John Howland, Richard Warren, Stephen Hopkins, Edward Dotey, John Allerton, Thomas English, Master Mate Clark, Master Gunner Copin and three sailors of the Mayflower Company.

How did the Mayflower navigate through Cape Cod Bay without getting stuck in the sandbars that stretch out far from shore during a low tide? Tides are extreme here—even more so during a full moon, when the beach appears to extend to the opposite shore across the bay with no water in sight. Whenever the tide is this low, I imagine it might be possible to walk the fifty miles directly north from First Encounter to Plymouth on the bottom of the bay.

If the tide had been low when the Puritans arrived here, they would have trudged ashore on the mucky bay floor, laden with their heavy woolen outerwear and their strides clumsy, particularly after being confined to the Mayflower for sixty-six days while crossing the Atlantic. Had the Nausets peered through the scrubby pines and tall beach grass that still grow along the bluffs and dunes as the Mayflower perused the coast? Or were they waiting on the beach when Miles Standish and the rest went ashore? And how foul these Englishmen must have smelled to the awaiting Nausets!

Less than a quarter of a mile out into the bay, a shipwreck sits upright with only its wooden hull intact. According to the owner of our rental cottage, it has been there for about a hundred years, though it seems ready to sail from the shallow cove of First Encounter Beach. With each summer we return, the relic grows smaller. Submersion in water preserves it, but at low tide, sun exposure causes the remaining structure to shrink—a ruin in constant preservation and decay, a visual conundrum. Once, at extreme low tide, I walked to it. As I was about to touch its encrusted moss and barnacle side, terror overtook me. Before I could overcome my fear, I was running back to shore, smashing mollusk beds with my bare feet.

IN "THE BLUE of Distance" from her collection of essays entitled *A Field Guide to Getting Lost*,[5] Rebecca Solnit describes how some white settlers, who had been captured by native people in the New World, remained with their Native American captors out of choice, particularly those who were taken as children and then adopted by the tribe as their own. In the recorded case of the former Puritan Eunice Williams, whose family had settled on Iroquois land in western Massachusetts, the tribe abducted her along with her older brother, Stephen. She was seven at the time. Stephen returned to their birth family after many years with the Iroquois family. Eunice did not. Her new family could not bear to give her up, because she had replaced one of their deceased children. Even so, it was Eunice who chose to remain with the Iroquois.

Solnit writes, "There is something obdurate, obsessive, inflexible about them [the Puritans], as hard and angular as conquistador's armor, as dreary as Puritan theology. The Iroquois were kinder to children, and perhaps the thing hardest for whites to accept, or often even to imagine, is that some captives preferred native culture." Her Puritan family deemed Eunice a tragic loss, but Solnit suggests otherwise. Eunice was no longer a captive because "she had become someone else." She was no longer waiting to return home; Eunice had found herself in this new identity.

SUNRAYS BEGAN TO heat my back; it was time to take one last shot of the plaque and avoid an overexposure. I looked through the viewfinder and focused, and then a voice called out to me, "Go to the dune to your right." I glanced up and saw a tall, willowy man pass in front of me a few feet away. He possessed androgynous features, like a Renaissance angel portrayed by Fra Lippo Lippi. His golden hair and striking blue eyes intensified his slight presence. An Australian border collie accompanying him ran over and sniffed my feet. Both man and dog projected an ethereal quality. Were these two real?

"Where?" I responded. Without stopping, he pointed his finger toward the sand dune as he and the dog vanished into the sea grass on my left.

I climbed the narrow footpath to the top of the dune. Almost hidden from view was another plaque, bolted to a granite boulder on the crest and overlaid with a sea-salt patina. It commemorated the same event but differently. At this monument, the native peoples were not portrayed as victims of their forthcoming doom. I knew the inscription might be difficult to read in a photograph, since the luster on the lettering had dissolved, but I took a shot of it anyway.

> ON THIS SPOT HOSTILE INDIANS HAD THEIR
> FIRST ENCOUNTER DECEMBER 8, 1620 WITH
> Myles Standish, John Carver, William Bradford,
> John Tilley, Edward Winslow,
> John Howland, Edward Tilley, Richard Warren, Stephen Hopkins,
> Edward Dotey, John Allerton, Thomas English, Master Mate Clark,
> Master Gunner Copin, and three sailors of the Mayflower Company.
> 1620 Provincetown Tercentary Commission 1920

I HAD THE film processed and printed upon returning home. Most of the roll was what I had expected. The photograph recording the gilded inscription of the plaque on the beach came out perfect; the lettering sharply glistened. The inscription on the plaque at the top of the dune, though correctly exposed, was mostly indecipherable.

But I had also captured something unexpected—an image of a group of tall, vertical shadows rising from the bottom of the photograph and extending horizontally across the beach. The photo gave the haunting illusion that a band of Nauset sentinels had stood with me, looking out at Cape Cod Bay as the tide returned to First Encounter Beach that morning.

ACKNOWLEDGMENTS

UNION LAKE WOULD not have come to fruition without the encouragement and support of Eileen Kitzis, whose writing classes were where my storytelling began; the graduate writing program at Sarah Lawrence College; my readers throughout the various stages of *Union Lake*; my editors, Emily Macel Theys, Mary Ann González, Adriana Stark, and Karen Clark; and my husband, Alex Stark.

ACKNOWLEDGMENT IS ALSO made to the following publications in which these works first appeared: "The First Encounter" in *Storyscape Literary Journal*, Issue 3, and "A Haircut in the Kitchen" in *Submerged: Tales from the Basin*, edited by Lauren González.

NOTES

1. Henry Miller, *Plexus: The Rosy Crucifixion* (New York: Grove Press, 1965), 1.
2. Miller, *Plexus*, 7.
3. Virginia Woolf, *To the Lighthouse* (London: J.M. Dent & Sons, 1955), 72.
4. Woolf, *To the Lighthouse*, 76.
5. Rebecca Solnit, *A Field Guide to Getting Lost* (New York: Viking Penguin, 2005), 74–75.

CARLA PORCH WAS raised on Union Lake in southern New Jersey. In addition to writing, she has spent many years working as a photographer, graphic designer, and art director. She lives in Venice, California.

CPSIA information can be obtained at www.ICGtesting.com
Printed in the USA
BVOW08s2223051213

338340BV00002B/117/P

9 781480 802155